D0592084

# administering
# change
# in schools

ROBERT G. OWENS
*School of Education*
*Brooklyn College, The City University of New York*

CARL R. STEINHOFF
*School of Education, Health, Nursing, and Arts Professions*
*New York University*

With a Foreword by Richard A. Schmuck

*Prentice-Hall, Inc. Englewood Cliffs, New Jersey*

*Library of Congress Cataloging in Publication Data*

OWENS, ROBERT G. (date)
  Administering change in schools.

  Bibliography: p. 169
  Includes index.
  1. School management and organization.  I. Stein-
hoff, Carl R. (date)  joint author.  II. Title.
LB2805.O83        371.2        75-22036
ISBN  0-13-004929-8

Printed in the United States of America

10  9  8  7  6  5  4  3  2  1

PRENTICE-HALL INTERNATIONAL, INC., LONDON
PRENTICE-HALL OF AUSTRALIA, PTY. LTD., SYDNEY
PRENTICE-HALL OF CANADA, LTD., TORONTO
PRENTICE-HALL OF INDIA PRIVATE LIMITED, NEW DELHI
PRENTICE-HALL OF JAPAN, INC., TOKYO
PRENTICE-HALL OF SOUTHEAST ASIA (PTE.) LTD., SINGAPORE

Lovingly dedicated to
GORONWY WILLIAM OWENS
and
ELLEN RUTH STEINHOFF

# contents

# foreword

I have read and reread this book and have found more and more useful concepts and recommendations in it with each new reading. It is superb in dozens of ways, both large and small, but there are three overarching themes that make this one of the very best texts available in educational administration. Succinctly stated, this book describes school organizations as they are today realistically and with a nice sense of proportion; it argues intelligently for what they ought to become; and it instructs administrators on how to change them.

Owens and Steinhoff present a down-to-earth description of the way schools operate as social systems along with a persuasive argument for the reason educational administrators should carefully attend to the systemic features of schools. They go on to present easily visualized group and organizational conditions toward which schools should be moving. And finally, they show school administrators how to use organizational theory and many of the concepts and techniques of organization development to ameliorate the systemic conditions of schools. Few texts for educational administrators have made concepts of planned organizational change so clear and practical.

For over a decade the discipline of educational administration has gradually, though haltingly, moved toward incorporating concepts and techniques of the applied social sciences. Most of these efforts at interdisciplinary integration have been isolated and small, usually with only a handful of participants. Even larger scientific explorations into school change have typically been carried out only by behavioral scientists and school consultants; practicing educational administrators usually have not been directly involved. Indeed, many of my recent contacts with school administrators indicate that there is a growing social distance between them and university-based social scientists.

With this text, Owens and Steinhoff have made a significant contribution to a rapprochement between educational administration and applied social science. They connect the fragments and the isolated contributions to school change made over the past two decades by social scientists and bring them together into an easy-to-follow, logical format. By so doing, they have created a very practical text for educators, while not compromising the high standards of academic social science.

Owens and Steinhoff are exemplary in their thorough coverage of scientific material on planned organizational change, leadership, motivation, and organization development; their lucid and easy-flowing writing style; and their attention to making complex concepts and techniques both understandable and practical. Along with the descriptions of the organizational circumstances of schools, some realistic systemic targets to work toward, and some tested paths of planned change, they also offer a sort of dictionary of applied social science for school administrators. Technical jargon is clearly defined and the annotated bibliographies help in clarifying the contributions from applied social science that have been particularly relevant to school administrators during the last decade.

I hope that this monumental effort toward an integration of the scholarly with the practical will be read by every practicing school administrator, by all aspirants to administrative positions in schools, and by many applied social scientists and school consultants.

RICHARD A. SCHMUCK
*Center for Educational Policy and Management*
*University of Oregon*

# preface

Our aim in this book is to provide the reader with a concise introduction to crucial knowledge and concepts that underlie the best contemporary approaches to the management of organizational change. We also provide the reader with suggestions for extending his or her search for knowledge in this area through further reading.

Our basic position is that one approach to the administration of change in schools is emerging as more successful than others. This approach is based upon knowledge about the nature of organizations and leadership that has been developed principally through the research and experience of behavioral scientists, especially since the decade of the 1950s. But, although that knowledge is basic to effective administration under modern conditions, it remains for the administrator to synthesize and draw selectively from it in confronting the tough practical problems that he or she routinely encounters in present-day schools.

In our judgment the central problem of school administration is to manage the schools so that they become increasingly better places in which our children may live, learn, and grow. In our fast-changing world, where change itself seems to be the only constant, this means that the problem actually centers around the management of planned change in schools. Because in our society many people play key roles in schools, this book may be useful to a wide audience: administrators and supervisors, as well as school board members, teachers and their organizational representatives, parents and parent organization members. Indeed, we are convinced that—while the administrator's role is clearly pivotal in bringing about change in schools—progress will be laboriously slow until community members and teachers develop a knowledgeable interest in the processes of organizational change.

These pages are the product of off-and-on collaboration between the authors over a span of a decade. In addition to teaching, that collaboration has included research and writing on different phases of the overall problem and consulting activities in a variety of schools: public and non-public, urban and suburban, as well as universities. During that time many people have helped to shape and develop our thinking: not least among these are our students in the graduate programs in Educational Administration at Brooklyn College, Cornell University, and New York University who, we suspect, have often been more helpful than they know.

We gratefully acknowledge the help, and often indulgence, of many colleagues both within and outside our respective universities who have shared their knowledge with us and have taken time to help us understand. Professor Richard A. Schmuck, of the Center for Educational Policy and Management at the University of Oregon, was particularly helpful by critically reading successive drafts of the manuscript. We are indebted, too, to Professor Lawrence L. Kavich, Chairperson of the Department of Educational Administration at Hofstra University, who provided us with many valuable suggestions after reading the manuscript. The senior author especially acknowledges the valuable contributions of Professor Helen Wardeberg, Chairperson of the Department of Education at Cornell University, other faculty members there, and many graduate students of that university who studied and critically discussed the manuscript while he was a visiting professor there.

We are indebted, too, to the many school teachers and administrators with whom we have worked over the years for their patience, their confidence, and the inspiration of their dedication.

We are especially grateful to the hundreds of Organization Development specialists throughout the United States and Canada not only for patiently providing us with information in response to our inquiries but also for taking a great deal of time and interest to correspond and share materials.

Finally, it is doubtful that this book would have been completed without the expert help so cheerfully given by Mrs. Pearl Friedman, Mrs. Elaine Golub, and Miss Shellie Owens in preparing successive drafts of the manuscript.

R.G.O.
C.R.S.

CHAPTER 1

# the problem of change in schools

In the mid-1970s, it was clear that the American public schools faced a crisis brought on by an increasing lack of public confidence that the schools could adequately respond to society's needs. In some cities the crisis appeared to be of very serious proportions; in other places, usually less urbanized, the problems were less intense. However, all across the nation school bond referenda were being defeated by voters at a record rate, school administrators were being dismissed or were resigning in record numbers, public educational alternatives to the public schools were being established with tax levy funds, and many Americans were seriously discussing the possibility of "deschooling" our society.[1] By 1975 declining enrollments in American public schools clearly heralded a new need for change that would be significant for years to come.

Clearly the schools—long notorious for their tendency to lag in adopting more effective practices—needed to solve the problems of changing in basic, significant ways if they were to regain the public confidence upon which their very survival depended.

To say that dealing with change is a major problem in the administration of public schools is to say nothing new. The pressure for change is constant and insistent; and, these days, it seems to come from all directions. Moreover, while faced with insistent demands that he effect meaningful change in the schools, the administrator is often surrounded by a plethora of proffered solutions to the problem at hand. It is a rare

[1] Ivan Illich, *Deschooling Society* (New York: Harper & Row, 1972).

1

active citizen or group that does not have a program to offer that claims to meet the need of the moment and the future.

In many ways schools have remained basically unchanged over the years as new programs and new materials have come and gone, and innovative approaches have proven to be ephemeral or disturbingly fragile. The history of American public schooling does not give rise to confidence that the schools are able to meet adequately the demand for change that they face today and that, in all probability, will increase in the future. Indeed, especially since the decade of the 1950s, the route that the American public schools have traveled is cluttered with the skeleton hulks of once-bright, new and promising programs of change long-since scuttled or junked. Teaching machines and language laboratories gather dust from coast-to-coast while many of the prepackaged curricula, hastily assembled at great expense in the 1950s, are ignored. Still, the ever-watchful public constantly expect educational administrators to produce answers to the demand for increased effectiveness of schools.

In response, new programs are seized upon, financed, and launched —nearly all to be accompanied by glowing reports of "success" and nearly all falling by the wayside within a few years. The result of this cyclic process has been a loss of public confidence in the presumed professional expertise of school administrators, with a diminishing of their authority and power. For example, legislation was enacted in several states in the early 1970s virtually eliminating educational credentials for certification of school superintendents. This action was eagerly approved by school board members across the country who were convinced that it would open the doors to a far more competent pool of talent than the trained and certificated educational administrators then represented.

## ASSESSING THE PROBLEM

The crucial part of solving a problem is to define it. It would be useful, then, for us to explore the problem of administering change in schools with the idea of clarifying its nature and dimensions.

*The demand for change is expressed in terms of problems to be solved; in the case of schools, these emerge—sooner or later—as issues of social policy.* To illustrate this in simple terms, we can consider the "Olde Deluder Satan Act" of 1647 by which the Massachusetts legislature initiated what is widely regarded as the first step toward compulsory education in Colonial America. In the preamble to that historic enactment, the legislature clearly stated the social issues that the new law was designed to meet: (1) to thwart Satan by providing an opportunity for all children to learn to read the Bible and (2) to assure that learning would be perpetuated beyond the first generation of settlers in the new land. As powerful and boldly innovative as this new approach to public schooling was, it posed relatively simple administrative and organizational problems. The new law clearly intended to provide literacy training and limited education to *certain* young people—those who wanted it and then only to the extent to which they were judged capable of profiting from it. No suggestion was made that the teacher or the school had any responsibility for the quality and extent of the child's achievement.

Thus was launched a relatively simple era of public schooling in America. Major issues centered around the extent to which opportunities for schooling should be made available to all children at public expense. Operational problems centered around offering opportunities for instruction to all while minimizing cost. How much a child learned, and how well, was considered to depend on discipline and the youngster's own ability.

This educational philosophy may be contrasted with that embodied in the Right to Read Program. In 1969 the U.S. Commissioner of Education expressed a new view of reading that has been compared in importance to the invention of movable type: the right to read. This new right, the right to read, it was claimed is fundamental to the right of life, liberty, and the pursuit of happiness. And the Right to Read—later endorsed and adopted by the President himself—was not limited to eliminating the last remnants of illiteracy in America: it was aimed at eliminating functional illiteracy in America by 1976. Basic reading skills, it was proclaimed, must be accompanied by the *desire* to read so that youth would, in fact, not only know how to read but would be stimulated to seek new knowledge and inspiration.

In enunciating this sweeping new right and setting a dazzling new goal for the schools, the Federal government went on to attack the schools and blame them for not already having done the job. For more than a quarter of the United States population who had been identified as having significant reading deficiencies it was claimed that education had been a failure and the call for immediate change was issued.

But unlike the Massachusetts enactment of 1647, no cue for correcting the problem was offered. When educators asked how to achieve the new goal, the Commissioner advised them not to get involved in debate over methods of teaching reading. His view was that we must be concerned with the goal, and not the details of teaching methods. The clear implication was that schools already knew how to achieve the goal but simply had not done the job. Noteworthy, too, is the strident egalitarian philosophy on which the Right to Read concept was based. Those who embraced the project's goals obviously believed that children do not differ intellectually in significant ways and that schools should recognize this—a different view of reality than the members of the Massachusetts General Court held in 1647.

In 1969, the same year as the Right to Read proclamation, the *Harvard Educational Review* printed Arthur Jensen's report on research concerning possible systematic intellectual differences between the cognitive functioning of black and white children. This was, of course, followed by great indignation because even to examine such possibilities ran counter to the rising egalitarian philosophy in America. It tended to weaken the increasingly popular notion that if a child failed to learn (to read, for example) the failure was due to the school's rather than the *child's* ability.

The Olde Deluder Satan Act of 1647 and the Right to Read promulgated 322 years later are typical examples of the way in which issues of social policy emerge to pose problems of change in the schools. For practical purposes, we shall divide these problems into two general types: *political problems* and *knowledge problems*.

## POLITICAL PROBLEMS

*A political problem is one that involves the gathering of sufficient public support to bring about a change in public policy.*

As late as the 1950s and even beyond, there was a widespread feeling among American school administrators that the public schools should somehow remain aloof from politics. However, it is being increasingly recognized by educators and others that the schools are really inextricably bound up in the political system of our society. The difficult job of interpreting the social issues of the day and relating them to what goes on in the schools can no longer be left exclusively to noneducators. The increasing demands of society that the schools become actively involved in the great issues of the time have challenged administrators to understand what is expected of them and to find ways of fulfilling these expectations.

*Educational administrators increasingly realize that schools that insulate themselves from the demands and pressures of citizens and interest groups are incapable of converting significant social issues into meaningful curricular and programmatic change.* Being at once responsible for the acquisition and allocation of school funds and subject to criticism for school deficiencies, administrators have become very sensitive to emerging social crises and highly responsive to federal and state initiatives to meet these problems.

The distribution of monetary resources determines the success or failure of a particular program. Efforts to attract additional money, which is the talisman of being on the "right" side in dealing with social issues, have increasingly tended to turn the administrators' attention to the Federal government. Because dealing with social issues is largely a political process, the administrator needs more than knowledge about American society and insight into its inner-workings. He needs contacts, access to early information, analytical skill, and an understanding of power and its effectiveness in dealing with other groups and organizations that are struggling for a share of the limited available resources.

By the beginning of the 1970s, school administrators were generally beginning to realize that, unless the public schools quickly learned to meet the public's expectations in dealing with social issues, other institutions and organizations might be asked to do the job.

To many it appeared likely that the American public schools were perilously close to bringing on their own demise. For if there is anything to be learned from the history of American public education, it is that an educational institution that ceases to meet the expectations of society will not survive.

*When schools are viewed as failing to deal effectively with problems arising from significant social issues of the time, they lose essential political support. Political influence is exerted on other agencies that, in turn, generate new programs that compete with public education.*

## KNOWLEDGE PROBLEMS

*A knowledge problem is one whose goals have been determined by public policy, but the means for achieving these goals are not clear.* Simply put, there is a clear-cut symbiotic relationship between the political pressures on education and the problem of finding ways to fulfill the desired social goals. Why is this so?

The answer lies in a belief that underlies our technological society: that which can be done must be done. One consequence of this view is that each new bit of knowledge that is invented or discovered creates additional pressures within the political system to achieve the social goals that this knowledge makes possible. Thus, it is becoming increasingly popular to see an analogy between the experience of the space program and the solution of other problems.

The story of that achievement—going from paper plans in the early 1960s straight to exploration of the moon by men and machines within a decade—is nothing short of mind-boggling. But what is frequently missed in attempts to apply the logic and process of that program to the solution of social problems is that, by the time the decision to go to the moon was made, virtually *all of the basic knowledge needed for doing it already existed.* Through centuries of careful scientific study and step-by-step development in many disciplines, a substantial body of knowledge had been developed, enabling scientists to forecast with remarkable clarity and accuracy just how to achieve their goals. In large measure, the problems confronting the space program—though far from trivial—were basically more of a technological nature than they were from a lack of knowledge.

By the 1970s, in fact, the accomplishments of the American space program—that had once had people literally sitting on the edge of their chairs—had become rather boring to many. But it would be interesting to speculate on what the public reaction might have been if, in the early 1970s, NASA had been forced to announce that after all their years of trying and all their billions of dollars expended they actually had not been able to get to the moon and had to acknowledge that they were not sure how to do the job. One can hardly imagine the bitterness of the disappointment, the outrage, the loss of prestige in the sciences, and the political consequences.

In dealing with education public administrators, political office-holders, and educational leaders are sometimes unaware of crucial knowledge problems that can block the way to achieving some highly desirable social goals. For example, at the time that he promulgated the politically tantalizing Right to Read Program, the United States Commissioner of Education appeared to be unaware that in practical terms the knowledge to achieve the lofty and desirable goals he set *simply did not exist beyond a primitive level.* Scientific workers from the behavioral disciplines had only filled in some of the knowledge gaps as to how reading is best learned and, therefore, taught. Lacking anything like a systematic knowledge base from which to draw, the literature in the field provided little more than a mixture of speculation, field studies, and experience that practitioners frequently found conflicting and confusing. Teachers—those responsible for synchronizing knowledge and practice—were consequently forced to improvise, gathering together as best they could those materials and methods that seemed to yield the best results in specific situations.[2] While the Commissioner had focused attention on the *goal,* that was basically political in nature, he had overlooked the essential fact that the *knowledge* necessary to achieve that goal had not yet been developed adequately.

On a broader, yet more intense scale, this same gap between aspirations born of politically attractive goals and the knowledge required for their achievement has been witnessed so frequently that public dis-

---

[2] Robert C. Aukerman describes one hundred ways to teach reading in *Approaches to Beginning Reading* (New York: John Wiley & Sons, Inc., 1971).

appointment in the "poor performance" of the schools has engendered deep frustration, bitterness, and alienation. In the 1960s, for example, one answer to race problems in America was to promise that the educational achievement of lower-class slum children would be raised by the schools. Skepticism from educators was brushed aside and the determination to reach the politically-desirable goal became paramount. As the struggle to achieve the goal intensified and success became elusive, bitterness and mistrust born of disappointment mounted. It was not unusual in communities throughout the country to place blame for failure on either the outright ineptitude of school teachers and administrators or the existence of a conspiracy on the part of middle-class teachers and administrators to foil the aspirations of their striving lower-class charges.

The Coleman report, that appeared in 1966 under the title "Equality of Educational Opportunity," was a major breakthrough in the knowledge problem that was actually blocking progress toward the goal that had been set for the schools. Essentially, this massive study changed our knowledge of how schools function: it was found that in some important ways schools functioned quite differently from the conventions of that time. Essentially, the Coleman report established three things:

1. There are great differences between the educational achievement of children based on ethnic and, by implication, social-class groups.
2. While there is variation in certain characteristics and resources of schools (e.g., class size, teacher credentials, per-pupil expenditure) from place to place across the country, the variation is not as great between rich and poor districts as was generally supposed.
3. Social-class status appears to predetermine the school achievement of children more than any other factor, and conventional inputs (such as per-pupil expenditure) have little effect on this.

Although some of these points are obvious, the Coleman report has brought to the attention of those concerned certain important aspects to consider in establishing educational reform toward more equal educational opportunity for all children, regardless of their ethnic or socioeconomic backgrounds. How this knowledge is to be used to bring about the desired educational changes has been the subject of much debate. Some people have concluded that "schools don't make any difference" and should be replaced by another form of educational enterprise. Others, working from the same facts, have concluded that schools *as they are presently constituted* do not make all the difference that we want in the educational attainment of different social groups, and this suggests that they should be changed in some way.

The knowledge problem involved in implementing clearly stated social or political educational goals is even more complex in many cases because not only are there many educational, social, and political goals that we do not know how to achieve through education but also—worse —few realize that we do not know how to achieve them. A bitter legacy developed in the 1960s because of this, rendering many of the problems inherited in the 1970s more difficult to solve. As schools failed to bring the achievement of lower socioeconomic-class children up to match the achievement of children from other groups, bitterness and resentment set in. Teachers and administrators were viewed as the tools of malevolent and contemptuous "outside" forces determined to ignore the needs, hopes, and desires of disadvantaged ethnic minority groups.

## ORGANIZATIONAL CHANGE: A KNOWLEDGE PROBLEM

Until recently deliberate attempts to plan, control, and direct change in organizations has had to be dealt with at the prescientific level. However, especially since World War II, scientific study of the enormously complex phenomena of organizational change has been developing very rapidly. One does not build a complete science in a quarter-century, of course, and—while much more is known about organizational change now than was known even a few years ago—our knowledge is still incomplete. Enough scientific work exists, however, to provide the administrative practitioner with some systematic concepts and insights on which to base decisions regarding practical problems. At the very least, enough scientific work has been done to enable the administrator to develop an orderly repertoire of strategies and tactics to utilize selectively in dealing with different situations.

### The Conventional Wisdom of Change

Typically, problems of directing and controlling change in schools have been approached in a relatively unsystematic way. Faced with the need for some kind of change in the school's goals or the way in which it seeks to attain its goals, the administrator tends to proceed more or less intuitively and falls back on common sense and his own experience. The results generally have been less than spectacular.

In part, this unhappy state of affairs stems from the fact that the folklore of change, as well as our own personal experiences with it, have much to tell us about ways of facilitating change in *individual persons* and very little about dealing with change as an *organizational* problem —which is the case in schools. Each of us generally tends to have a limited perspective of change and how to deal with it. This is not to belittle in any way the importance of the individualistic aspects of the problems of dealing with change.

Indeed, a great deal of existing theory and knowledge concerning change and how to deal effectively with it is, in fact, focused on the problems of individuals: how new ideas spread, what makes some people accept change while others do not, and how to facilitate the more rapid utilization of new ways or the adoption of new goals by significant numbers of people.

Generally conservative, tradition-bound, and poorly educated, farmers around the world have been the subject of extensive research in their confrontation with the need to change. It became clear long ago that such technological breakthroughs as the development of new seeds or new knowledge concerning the use of fertilizers tended to have little impact on the ways that farmers usually did things. Skeptical of new ideas, farmers have tended to cling to the methods and procedures that they know best: they have persisted in using techniques that "work" rather than experimenting in some new ways. How, then, do we bring about a "green revolution"—getting farmers to plant new crops and grow them in new ways so as to increase significantly per-acre yield and reduce the production cost?

### A Strategy for Individual Change

Significant numbers of farmers now recognize that certain key steps are involved in moving an idea from the drawing board to its adoption.

1. *Dissemination*—there must be channels of communication to spread knowledge of the new idea swiftly and accurately. In American farming the Agriculture Experiment Stations and Extension Programs have often served as vehicles for disseminating new ideas rapidly across the country.
2. *Demonstration*—demonstrations of the new practice have been conducted under actual conditions in convenient locations to make it possible for farmers to see first-hand what the new idea is and how it can be used.
3. *Adoption*—by getting key local farmers (whose neighbors respect them and look up to them as important people) to adopt the new idea, more cautious and reluctant farmers tend to want to follow suit.
4. *Technical assistance*—practical, detailed "how-to-do-it" help to the local farmer must be provided to make his early attempts fruitful. In American agriculture this service has often been supplied by the County Agricultural Agent.

This proven route to change in agriculture has been demonstrated repeatedly as it has radiated from the Western world to the so-called underdeveloped nations. The 1970 Nobel Peace Prize, awarded to agronomist Norman E. Borlaug for his contributions to increased cereal production in such places as Mexico and India, rested not only on the "genetic engineering" of the scientist but also on the proven methods that translated his scientific work from laboratory studies to a new approach to cereal production around the world. The fact that within ten years of his arrival in Mexico that nation stopped importing wheat and ten years after that was averaging a yield of thirty-nine bushels per acre (as against its previous eleven-bushel-per-acre yield) was not exclusively due to his new seeds. Along with the use of the new seed strains, farmers had to learn about controlled irrigation, pesticides and insecticides, mechanization, and improved marketing and storage facilities. Thus, the well-developed change tactics that have become familiar to farmers of Western nations have enabled farmers elsewhere to expand their wheat production in a relatively short time, providing more food for the hungry populations of the underdeveloped nations.

### Applying Individual Change Strategy to Schools

Serious research efforts to discover a parallel between the change model typified by agriculture and the problems of schools have been undertaken. However, the analogy between a school system and a farmer is, at best, imperfect. It is possible, of course, to view the school administrator as the key person in the school system and thus to link him and his behavior with the performance of the entire system. It has been found, for example, that school superintendents who frequently are exposed to new ideas by attending meetings and participating in conferences and by visiting other school districts tend to be early adopters of new ideas.[3]

Usually such superintendents are admired by their colleagues. They are likely to learn of new ideas early and see them in practice before many of their colleagues do. Since their views carry weight with their fellow superintendents, the fact that the early adopters lean toward a new idea helps to convince those who might be reluctant.

Regardless of how captivated a school administrator may be by a new idea, the real test of change in schools rests on the extent to which the organization—the school system and the individual schools—moves to put the idea into practice. Thus we have an organizational problem —one with which individual adopters, such as farmers, have little concern. Clearly the school administrator has great influence over change

3 See, for example, Richard O. Carlson, *Adoption of Educational Innovations* (Eugene, Oregon: Center for the Advanced Study of Educational Administration, University of Oregon, 1965).

practices in the school district. If he or she favors an idea, its chances of being put into action are greatly enhanced. The administrator who opposes an idea has great power to keep it from flourishing in the schools of the district. Conversely, teachers traditionally have had very limited power to move the organization to change in significant ways. While the administrator can pave the way for major changes, such as open enrollment or district-wide busing, teachers and teacher committees usually have been limited to such changes as the rearrangement of courses and course content.

Usually in an organization, then, the ideas of people in the higher echelons carry more weight and are acted upon more readily than the ideas of those in lower positions. This state of affairs has nothing whatever to do with the *quality* of the ideas that the organization acts upon. Indeed, as we have all seen at one time or another in our own experience good ideas of lower-echelon people are frequently ignored in favor of poorer ideas advanced by higher-echelon individuals. In dealing with *organizational* change one must confront the realities of traditional organizational life, such as the conventional top-to-bottom orientation with which most of us have learned to view organizations wherein ideas are supposed to be born at the top and passed down the line to be implemented.

However, even a casual observer is frequently struck by the disparity between what may be described as the rhetoric of many school-district administrators and the day-to-day experience encountered by pupils and students in the schools. New, perhaps innovative, programs are announced and funded but—all too often—in the end they are quietly phased out or merged with existing programs or abandoned for some new "breakthrough" innovation that will supposedly finally solve the problem.

### The Problem of Organizational Change

The problem—essentially an organizational one—is shared by schools as well as many other kinds of organizations, such as business firms, military organizations, universities, labor unions, and government agencies. The problem is one of moving and shaping an entire organization—from its top policy-making level to its operations level—to initiate, implement, utilize, adopt, and make workable the changes that are needed to achieve the organization's objectives. Many observers have despaired at the seeming obdurate nature of various organizations: their tendency to maintain a sort of equilibrium defies meaningful change.

To one concerned with bringing about reform in schools, then, it becomes necessary to consider not merely the development of innovative educational ideas and technological means for implementing them but the organizational aspects of the problem. Teachers work within complex organizations and are therefore constrained in their professional practice by the culture of the organizations. For that reason the focus of change efforts must be directed as much on the organization as on the individual teachers who depend on the organization in their practice. The primary target of change efforts in education is not *teachers* at all but is the *organizational system* itself.

This is, of course, antithetical to the folklore of educational administration that tends to assume that given teachers who are more pedagogically expert, the school will be more effective as an organizational system. Thus, we chronically find every incoming crop of new college graduates being viewed as inadequately trained for their work. To correct this defect, teachers become the targets of (1) orientation programs, (2) close, detailed supervision, and (3) inservice training. These processes, it is reasoned, will develop higher levels of on-the-job performance and will also encourage teachers to adopt new teaching methods and techniques that will ultimately make the school more effective in reaching its goals.

This approach is not a model for organizational change at all, but rather can be remarkably effective in *maintaining* the school's goals and the processes by which it attempts to achieve those goals.

## THE HARWOOD MANUFACTURING COMPANY CASE

A classic case in the literature of organizational change is that of the Weldon Manufacturing Company—the quality leader in men's pajamas that was probably headed for bankruptcy when it was taken over by the Harwood Manufacturing Company.[4]

Weldon's problems were not of a technical or technological nature: the firm was the acknowledged style and quality leader in its field with a well-earned market and a substantial production and distribution organization. In fact, few people knew more about the men's pajama business than the two partners who headed the Weldon firm. Their problem, it turned out, was managerial—or, as school people would say, administrative. They were having serious difficulties in managing the need for constant change with which all modern industrial and business enterprises are faced. On the other hand, while the people at Harwood Manufacturing Company knew a great deal about the pajama business, they were also highly knowledgeable about the management of change processes

---

4 This case is often referred to in the literature. See especially Alfred J. Marrow, David G. Bowers, and Stanley E. Seashore, *Management by Participation* (New York: Harper and Row, 1967).

in organizations and were able to apply this knowledge profitably to the Weldon firm.

To effect the needed changes at Weldon the management of the Harwood Manufacturing Company applied the concepts that underlie what is now known as *participative management*. A basic concept of participative management is that organizations make better decisions when the work groups most affected by the consequences of the decision are actively involved in (a) identifying the problem and (b) deciding what should be done. This approach is a direct application of contemporary motivation theory and social systems theory, especially as expressed in the work of Kurt Lewin, Abraham Maslow, Frederick Herzberg, and Douglas McGregor.

Conventional management approaches would have dictated that management should have first decided what the problems were and how to solve them, then proceed to retrain the workers and redirect their efforts toward greater productivity. Instead, the Harwood management went to the workers and asked *them* what the problems were and how to solve them. They then did their best to coordinate and implement the workers' ideas. This was a pioneer effort to develop new techniques of industrial management adapted to current needs and conditions; the source of the new techniques was not to be found in past experience but had to be drawn from behavioral science knowledge. Such techniques are now widely used in all highly industrialized nations of the world.

The lessons to be drawn from this as well as many other similar cases are not limited to manufacturing firms. Indeed, they bring into question some of the most cherished and traditional beliefs and concepts of managers and administrators of virtually all kinds of organizations.

## SUMMARY

Problems of change in education fall into two broad categories:

1. *political problems,* involving the establishment of educational goals as public policy, and
2. *knowledge problems,* involving the knowledge of how to achieve a goal that has been established.

The lag that schools have displayed in meeting the changing goals demanded of them has resulted in great loss of public confidence; if protracted, it could result in a shifting of resources to new organizations that appear more likely to achieve the goals.

Educational administrators have been heavily influenced to believe that increased expenditure and organizational expansion is basic to improved organizational functioning. Current keen competition for limited financial resources requires rethinking of policies of organizational incrementalism and finding more effective ways to utilize existing resources. The administrator must review his organization in the hope of finding better ways of redirecting existing resources into new, more productive enterprise.

*The administrator is concerned primarily with knowledge problems involved in administering change in schools,* rather than issues concerning the kind or direction of change that public policy may require. We seek to help the administrator to better understand schools as organizations and attempt to suggest to him how to direct and control these changes in a systematic and planned way. With a repertoire of organizational change strategies and tactics based upon recently-developed scientific knowledge, concept, and theory, the administrator will be in a position to provide stronger and more flexible educational leadership in meeting the emerging demand for dynamic change-oriented schools.

The Harwood Manufacturing Company case illustrates the application of concepts of participative management in which management facilitates the efforts of work groups to identify problems, decide upon effective action, and work cooperatively with management and organizational specialists to improve the functioning of organizations. Such an approach not only seeks to optimize the full resources and energies of all the people in the organization to achieve organizational goals by involving them meaningfully in the processes of problem solving, but also demands a new approach to leadership. Whereas it was once well-accepted that administration's role was to generate solutions to organizational problems and communicate them down the line to be implemented by teachers and students, it is now clear that broader participation promises greater payoff. In an era of rising professionalism among teachers, increased concern for human dignity and achievement, and declining coercive power of educational administrators over their subordinates, participative administration offers a new dimension of leadership to administrators. It also calls for new views of administrative leadership and the development of appropriate concomitant skills.

## SUGGESTED READING

Each of the following authors, in the work suggested and in other writings, has provided fundamental impetus to the development of concepts which underlie contemporary understanding of administering change in schools. While the suggested readings in this chapter do not specifically deal with schools, the insights which they convey have obvious implications for the administration of schools. All of the authors have extensive backgrounds of active involvement in solving practical problems in complex organizations.

HERZBERG, FREDERICK. *Work and the Nature of Man.* Cleveland: The World Publishing Company, 1966. Suggests an insight to motivation of people at work which challenges well-established views of administrators and describes their implications for leadership and supervision.

LEWIN, KURT. "Frontiers in Group Dynamics," *Human Relations,* I (1947), 5–41. The basis for contemporary understanding of participative methods of organizational change was largely laid down by Lewin and his students. In this classic work Lewin describes crucial underlying concepts with elegant clarity.

McGREGOR, DOUGLAS. *The Professional Manager.* New York: McGraw-Hill, 1967. McGregor is credited by many with pioneering the systematic application of behavioral science to a strategy for management, which he describes in this book.

MASLOW, ABRAHAM. *Motivation and Personality,* 2nd ed. New York: Harper & Row, 1970. Basic reading for anyone seriously interested in administration. Maslow's concept of motivation has had deep impact upon contemporary organizational psychology.

# CHAPTER 2

# administration, change, and schools

Words convey concepts and meaning that are the key to understanding. Often such words as *administration, change,* and *schools* are so commonly used that our understanding of them becomes imprecise. It is worthwhile, therefore, for us to take a brief look at these key words to see how they are used in this discussion.

## ADMINISTRATION

The term *administration* is generally used when referring to the management of governmental or institutional affairs. *Management* is the preferred term when discussing the administration of profit-oriented organizations. Though some educators shun the latter term as having an authoritarian connotation unsuitable for schools, the terms are synonymous for practical purposes. Administration is defined here, after Hersey and Blanchard's definition of management, as *working with and through individuals and groups to accomplish organizational goals.*[1]

The resources that the administrator uses, both human and material, are finite; hence, their effective deployment and utilization are persistent central concerns for administrators. Since the administrator is effective largely to the extent to which he can exercise leadership in

---

[1] Paul Hersey and Kenneth H. Blanchard, *Management of Organizational Behavior* (Englewood Cliffs, N.J.: Prentice-Hall, Inc., 1972), p. 3.

working with and through other people, concern for the social processes of coordinated human effort is very important. However, his ultimate concern is always to achieve the goal set forth by the organization. Organizational goals are variously called objectives, missions, purposes, tasks, and functions.

### Science and Administration

Traditionally, administration has been practiced and taught largely as an art. "The men of experience spoke to the novices of what they had found successful in the course of their careers. Frequently, the advice was embellished with general principles and basic truths, but the burden of the argument was pragmatic, and the burden of the evidence was buried irretrievably beneath the trials and errors of day-to-day management." [2] In this view, then, broad on-the-job experience plus certain personal characteristics (e.g., common sense and the ability to get along with people) were seen as basic elements for success in administrative practice.

Since World War II there has been a prodigious increase in the scientific development of knowledge and theory concerning organizations now known as *organization theory*. This field of study cuts across a number of disciplines upon which administration science is based. The fields of study that have contributed most to the development of organization theory are architecture, business administration, economics, education, engineering, law, political science, psychiatry, social psychology, cybernetics, sociology, and statistics.

Scientists and scholars concerned with organizations—whatever their basic disciplines may be—share a language, a set of concerns, and a gestalt of theory and concept. These enable them to communicate and mutually to build a body of scientific knowledge concerning organizations and their administration. *Thus we have an increasingly expanding body of knowledge that cuts across specific kinds of organizations and is generally applicable to the administration of various kinds of organizations: profit-oriented, military, educational, and governmental institutions.* The science of administration—still in its early stages of development—is being built largely upon the knowledge base provided by organization theory.

Contemporary administration is, necessarily, a mix of art and science. The science is still incomplete, and so our knowledge is limited. Lacking a complete scientific knowledge base for everything he deals with, the administrator frequently calls upon his own past experience or simply his intuition as a guide to action. With the rapid growth and

---

[2] James G. March, "Introduction" in James G. March, ed., *Handbook of Organizations* (Chicago: Rand McNally & Company, 1965), p. xiii.

maturity of the disciplines that have contributed most to administrative science since World War II, however, there has been a marked increase in the knowledge base with a consequent decrease in the need for wholly intuitive approaches to administrative problems. In broad terms, administrators utilize two kinds of knowledge in their professional practice: (1) the specialized technical knowledge involved in the operations of a specific organization, and (2) the more generally applicable knowledge that relates to administration as a general practice.

Every administrator must possess sufficient technical knowledge and skills to enable him to work effectively with others in achieving the goals of the organization, no matter what kind of organization it is. School administrators are no exception and need to deal knowledgeably with many technical areas of vital concern to the operation of the schools: from the intricacies of property taxation to methods of grouping children for instruction, from the ever-changing law on education to school-community relations, from tests and measurement of learning to the latest thinking on the cognitive development of children. This kind of knowledge is specialized and, therefore, we would not normally expect to find it widely shared by administrators in nonschool organizations.

But all administrators share at least one thing in common. Since, by definition, administration takes place in organizations, the effectiveness of administrators depends in large measure on their knowledge of organizations as well as their specialized technical knowledge and skills. They must be aware of how and why they function as they do and should be able to predict the effect of given alternative administrative actions. It is the continual study of these kinds of issues in a wide variety of organizations that gives promise of reducing trial-and-error in conducting organizational affairs and will lead to the development of a science of administration. This is the area in which the work of social and behavioral scientists has been especially helpful.

### Behavioral Science and Administration

The disciplines that have been most productive in the development of modern administrative practice are psychology (especially social psychology), psychiatry, sociology, and social anthropology. However, the behavioral aspects of political science, economics, and biology have also been fruitful sources of knowledge. Administrators and managers in many fields—hospitals, business, schools, the military, churches, and many others—have drawn upon the work of behavioral scientists for concepts and knowledge to guide them to improved administrative practice in dealing with their organizations. There is an increasingly expanding body of administrative knowledge that cuts across specific kinds of organizations and is thought to be generally applicable to various kinds of organizations. Thus a discipline of administration based on knowledge developed through scientific procedures and seen as applicable in a variety of organizations is being developed.

Although contributions from the behavioral sciences are still fragmentary, they have opened horizons in the search for new solutions to vexing organizational problems. For example, when the management of Harwood Manufacturing Company set out to solve the problems of the Weldon Company, they turned to a group of psychologists who had considerable experience in dealing with organizational problems instead of calling in only experts in the technology of clothing manufacture. These scientists were able to make a number of specific suggestions about Weldon's organization and work practices. When implemented, these changes improved the performance of the company rather quickly, so that it not only avoided bankruptcy but once more became a profitable and growing business. This theme is being repeated with increasing frequency as managers and administrators become more sophisticated in their use of behavioral science knowledge and concepts in solving organizational problems.

### The Theory Problem

It has frequently been observed that there is a strong antitheory bias in education or, as Theodore Sizer expresses it, an *anticonceptualization bias*.[3] In dealing with problems of organizational change, for example, it is unusual to hear education administrators discussing *theories* of change or *concepts* of overall change strategies. They seem more concerned with describing examples of change efforts. When school people meet to talk about change-oriented problems they rarely discuss a basic theoretical concept underlying their views. Instead, they tend to say, "Let me tell you what we are doing" and then go on to describe a program that may or may not have relevance to the situations their colleagues are facing.

School administrators tend to be action-oriented people, *doers.* Typically, they see themselves as people pitted against the harsh relentless realities of the "real" world who must *act,* must get things done, and have little time for theorizing—which is often seen as the plaything of dreamy philosophers or scholars safely sheltered in some ivory tower. Viewed in this way, theory may be seen as some sort of ideal state unrelated to reality or an expression of "the way things ought to be."

The scientist, on the other hand, tends to view theory as bedrock

[3] Theodore Sizer, "Three Major Frustrations: Ruminations of a Retiring Dean," *Phi Delta Kappan,* LIII, No. 10 (June, 1972), pp. 632–35.

fundamental in any effort to improve things. In his view, theory is no idle dream; it is a hard-headed way of thinking about reality that enables one to understand that reality better, describe it more accurately, and develop ways of dealing with it. An attempt to conceptualize a theoretical approach to an organizational problem is really an attempt to create an accurate model of reality—a statement that represents the essence of reality stripped of the distracting "sound and fury" possibly present in any specific school situation.

Armed with a good theoretical concept of organizations, it is possible to analyze specific situations in coherent terms and predict the outcome of proposed administrative action. By the patient process of building, testing, and relating various theoretical approaches to administration the scientist and the administrator move beyond the time-honored tradition that looked to innate shrewdness and first-hand experience for insight to important problems. The aim is to develop a more extensive repertoire of administrative style and action geared to a more accurate perception of reality than we have had in the past.

The essential contribution of science to the school administrator, in terms of practical application to the actual running of schools, has been the development of a deeper, more basic, conceptualization of organizational problems. When applied thoughtfully and systematically in practice this approach has led to fundamentally different approaches to the problem of administering change in organizations, with the following principal effects:

1. It has provided a multiplicity of clearly different approaches to the problem of change in organizations, each with appropriate procedures and processes for implementation, from which the administrator can deliberately select.
2. It has permitted the administrator to plan a program of organizational change with a scope and overall coherence and consistency not possible under more intuitive approaches.

But the administration of schools cannot be left to the behavioral or social scientist, much as some scientists would wish it so. The scientist, even the applied social scientist, is not, after all, an administrator. His contributions deal with only part of the challenge that the practicing administrator faces. While it cannot be denied that social science concepts and knowledge have had fundamental impact on administration, we must also bear in mind that the administrator deals with a much broader range of technical knowledge and skills than the behavioral and social sciences encompass.

Thus, the administrator draws from the behavioral and social sciences the concepts that seem useful in terms of successful administrative practice and blends them with the knowledge and skills he draws from other relevant disciplines.

## CHANGE

Certainly one of the dominant themes of our life and times is change; its pervasiveness, its rapid pace, its effect on traditional practices, ethics, beliefs, and behavior are familiar challenges to everyone. Because *change* is one of the most frequently used words in the literature on organization, as well as elsewhere, it is not surprising that it often seems to lack clarity (if not precision) in use.

Organizations that are structured and administered in traditional fashion tend to be highly resistant to change. Every school administrator is familiar with the charge that, despite the introduction of new programs, the schools do not really change. In this fast-changing world there are few organizations that can stand untouched by change. When a school introduces a new course, or reorganizes an old course, or rearranges its way of grouping students for instruction, or adds a preschool program, can we consider these meaningful changes? And if they are not, then what are they?

### Organizational Change

One way of dealing with this problem is to differentiate between relatively superficial adaptations and fundamental change.

*Organizational change* is a specific term that refers to fundamental changes in the organization. It is used when referring to an alteration of the existing state of *more than one* of the following aspects of the organization: (1) its tasks, (2) its structure, (3) its technology, or (4) its people.[4] Although less fundamental alterations in the organization may appropriately enough be described as changes in the popular sense, they do not represent what we call *organizational change*. In too many cases, claims to change in schools have been based on relatively superficial tinkering. Fundamental organizational change involving the four organizational factors enumerated above should result in demonstrably changed

---

[4] The four organizational factors upon which this analysis is based are explained by Harold J. Leavitt in "Applied Organizational Change in Industry: Structural, Technological and Humanistic Approaches" in James G. March, ed., *Handbook of Organizations* (Chicago: Rand McNally & Company, 1965).

capability of the organization to diagnose its basic problems with regard
to the classic criteria of efficiency and effectiveness.[5]

*Organizational drift* probably accounts for more claims to change
in schools and other organizations than most administrators would be
willing to admit. The term connotes, of course, a sort of unplanned
"drifting with the tide" adaptation to the overwhelming forces of change
that permeate the environment in which the schools function. Conversely,
contemporary concepts of organizational change include a significant
element of deliberateness that involves planning, direction, and control
of the attempt to bring about fundamental alteration of the organization. We shall use the terms *change* and *organizational change* in this
book to refer to planned, systematic controlled efforts to alter more than
one of the following aspects of the organization: (1) its tasks. (2) its
structure, (3) its technology, or (4) its participants in ways thought to
increase organizational efficiency and effectiveness.

### Innovation

Innovation is a form of change that represents some new relationship between ideas or concepts, the outcome of which may be predictable
but contains some element of the unknown and is not generally regarded
as standard practice. For example, if a traditionally graded elementary
school should adopt or implement some sort of continuous progress plan
to replace the older system of grouping children by grade, it would undoubtedly be thought of as an organizational change; it would be (1) a
planned, systematic change that would be intended to be more effective
in achieving the school's goals, and (2) it would alter at least the structure
and key human factors of the school as an organization. But could it
properly be called an innovation? Probably not, because continuous progress plans have been widely adopted in elementary schools and can therefore no longer be considered innovative.

A second difference between organizational change in general and
innovation is the characteristic of specificity generally associated with
innovation. According to Miles, ". . . the element of specificity might
easily be labeled 'thingyness'; innovations in education . . . ordinarily
have a defined, particular, specified character . . .".[6] In a sense, then,
innovation is usualy *an* innovation: a thing, as Miles points out, a
"package," a clearly related set of operational procedures and accom-

[5] *Efficiency* refers to the ability of the organization to attract and maintain the
involvement of participants; *effectiveness* refers to the extent to which the organization achieves its goals. See Chester I. Barnard, *Functions of the Executive*
(Boston: Harvard University Press, 1938).
[6] Matthew B. Miles, *Innovation in Education* (New York: Columbia University,
1964), p. 14.

panying technology. In this vein, then, we can list innovations by name, aware that the knowledgeable reader will quickly associate a specific, clearly describable set of practices and materials that go with each name. In that sense, each of the following was an innovation at one time or another: the Dalton Plan, Head Start, Kindergarten, the British Infant School, the Carnegie Unit, and Individually Prescribed Instruction.

### Product or Process

One may conceptualize change in organizations as either a *product* or a *process*. A popular view is to stress the product aspect: the adoption and utilization of some new product or invention. Examples of this abound in the numerous attempts to introduce the so-called Open Classroom concept in American elementary schools beginning in the early 1970s. As it was conceptualized and translated into operational terms by various educators, it was regarded as a product: it was specific, definable, describable and in that sense was a "thing." The goal in many schools became one of instituting this teaching concept in operational terms that included a specified set of behavioral norms, and physical arrangements in the classrooms thought to facilitate the achievement of those norms. The organizational change problem became one of introducing this innovative product as a standard mode of operation in place of whatever mode had previously been the normative standard for pupil and teacher behavior in that school. In organizational and administrative terms, this is the problem of the *adoption* of change.

Process-oriented students of organizational change tend to place the adoption of any given new technique or product into long-term perspective and view it as only one event in the ongoing life of the organization. This view emphasizes the functioning of the organization as a problem-solving, adaptive system whose existence and operation contribute to the maintenance of a high level of goal achievement or, better yet, facilitate the improvement of goal achievement over time. In this sense, focus is not on the adoption of *a single* change or innovation. *The focus is on very practical administrative problems having to do with the processes by which decisions are made in the organization, and ways one can improve the quality of the decisions that are made.*[7]

[7] In the case of the Weldon Manufacturing Company, that we have described, the essence of the change effort was to modify the processes through which decisions were reached regarding work practices. Instead of making the decisions at top management level and passing them down the line to be implemented, the new process involved lower-level participants in meaningful ways in the identification and solving of problems of basic importance to them as well as to the organization. The key to improving the goal-achievement of the organization was viewed as the development of more effective ongoing processes of decision-making rather than the adoption of some new work technology.

As the term *adoption of change* suggests, one of the basic assumptions of such an approach to organizational change is that some sort of invention—in terms of the organization's tasks, its structure, or technology, or involving the organization's people—exists that appears to be desirable in terms of facilitating a higher level of achievement of the organization's goals, and therefore should be adopted. Whatever that invention is—perhaps differentiated staffing, or flexible modular scheduling, or closed circuit television, or a compensatory education program—if it involves fundamental organizational change, then the problems involved in adopting it place heavy demands on the organization and are a challenge to the administrator's skills in dealing with the *processes* of organizational change.

## ORGANIZATIONAL ASPECTS OF SCHOOLS

Max Weber's analysis of organizations effectively stated the assumptions that have generally guided thinking about organizations during the first half of this century, and, according to Amitai Etzioni, still accounts for most of contemporary analysis of formal organizations.[8] Weber, a leading European sociologist writing in the early part of the century, was concerned about the development of large-scale organizations to meet conditions arising from the technological and industrial revolution, with its concomitant political and social changes.

At that time, the primitive state of scientific knowledge of organization gave little guidance to those who were seeking to improve organizational performance. Their inheritance from the past, however, was dominated by what Weber called (1) *charismatic* organizations or (2) *traditional* organizations. In the charismatic organization, the authority system was largely based on the personal charisma of a leader. The traditional organization, as Weber thought of it, had an authority system based on inherited position: one of noble rank, or of a privileged caste or class, such as the European concept of a feudal landowner.

### Bureaucracy

Bureaucracy offers an organizational alternative that stresses *rationality* (rather than *personality*), legally-established systematic relationships between offices, an orderly hierarchical distribution of power and authority, and the assurance that positions will be filled on the basis of

---

[8] Amitai Etzioni, *Modern Organizations* (Englewood Cliffs, N.J.: Prentice-Hall, Inc., 1964), p. 31.

competence. All of these elements are brought together in the authority system that bureaucracy utilizes. Its essence is rationality: the entire organization is developed and administered in accordance with logic and system as applied to the work and goals of the organization.

A bureaucracy divides the work into specialized phases according to some rational, logical plan that has been devised by experts. Each phase of the work is performed by trained specialists who have demonstrated their competence to do the work well, usually through some preemployment examination procedure. The whole system is controlled and coordinated by logically developed written rules, policies, and procedures promulgated by specialists. These rules, in a sense, are the law of the organization.

Success in achieving the organization's goals is seen as depending in large measure upon the fidelity with which this rational-legal arrangement is applied in actual practice. Deviations from the established rules, policies, and procedures are generally viewed as aberrations that tend to threaten the integrity of the system.

Ideally the bureaucrat is trained to deal with facts and ignore personal appeals for exceptions no matter how emotionally tinged they may be. He is also expected to ignore his own personal feelings in applying the rules to a specific situation; they are irrelevant and potentially harmful in the overall functioning of the system. One must differentiate between a given office or position in a bureaucracy and the person who happens to occupy that position.

Thus one can view a bureaucratic organization as a relatively permanent structure comprised of an interrelated set of offices; each office is assigned certain circumscribed tasks to be performed and rules to govern their performance. Those occupying these offices may be viewed as relatively temporary incumbents; they have no personal claim to their positions or the power and authority that goes with them. The offices of a bureaucracy are arranged in a systematic hierarchy, with the higher offices supervising the work of the lower offices. The concept is one in which power and authority are distributed in the organization by policies and rules that assign it. There is a powerful element of control exercised asymmetrically from the top down which is strongly reinforced by (1) cultivating emphasis on status differences according to rank of office in the hierarchy, and (2) placing control of the system's rewards (tenure, promotion, access to physical facilities) exclusively in the hands of those in higher authority. Thus the hierarchical arrangement of the bureaucracy provides an enduring system for the maintenance of control and discipline by (1) stressing the legal authority of a higher-echelon person (emphasizing the use of titles, assignment of office space and prerogatives

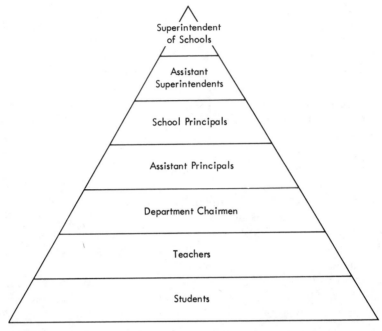

**Figure 2-1**
A typical illustration of the pyramidal form of organization as applied to a
school district.

according to rank, and careful attention to protocol), and (2) putting
lower-echelon persons in a state of continuous dependence upon their
superiors in order to "get ahead."

The pyramidal hierarchy lends itself very readily to the implementation of certain fundamental principles of bureaucratic organization and administration that are directly related to the decision-making
processes of the organization:

1. As a decision becomes more complex, takes on a broader scope, and
   becomes more important to the organization, responsibility for making
   the decision should be shifted upward to higher levels of authority.
2. Disagreements between individuals and groups who are on the same
   level should be resolved by the superior in the hierarchy to whom those
   individuals or groups report.
3. Communication should be restricted to the established official channels
   that link the hierarchical levels.

These notions are no artifacts incidental to any natural laws of organizational life; they are inventions of man based on significant funda-

mental principles or value judgments that go far in defining how a
bureaucracy is organized and how it functions.

By controlling the channels through which the bureaucrat may seek
to influence higher levels of the system, the bureaucracy can easily
minimize the influence of lower-level participants in the overall functioning of the organization. Embodied in or supported by the hierarchical
arrangement of the bureaucracy, such functional principles serve to
create a very strong, very durable authority system with powerful top-to-
bottom orientation.

However, "bureaucratic organizations are more than mere devices
for producing goods or services. They have critical normative consequences. They provide the environment in which most of us spend our
lives. In their efforts to rationalize human energy they become sensitive
and versatile agencies for the control of man's behavior, employing subtle
psychological sanctions that evoke desired responses and inculcate con-
sistent patterns of action" [9] and thus shape the behavior and thought of
their participants in countless ways. One of the consequences of this is
to develop behavior patterns that exaggerate the characteristic patterns
required by bureaucratic performance.

Though he clearly saw these problems, Weber described the
"technical superiority" of bureaucracy "over any other form of organization" thus:

> The fully developed bureaucratic mechanism compares with other organi-
> zations exactly as does the machine with the non-mechanical modes of
> production.
> Precision, speed, unambiguity, knowledge of the files, continuity, dis-
> cretion, unity, strict subordination, reduction of friction and of material
> and personal costs—these are raised to the optimum point in the strictly
> bureaucratic organization . . .[10]

Notice that Weber said nothing about change, adaptability, flexibility,
or developing creative solutions to the organization's problems. Such an
organizational system creates a characteristic social structure and a
genotypic psychological climate conducive to evoking highly predictable
behavior by the participants.

However, as James G. Anderson has pointed out,

> in attempting to structure and impersonalize relationships so as to mini-
> mize the influence of the individual on the accomplshment of organiza-

9 Robert Presthus, *The Organizational Society* (New York: Alfred A. Knopf,
Inc., 1962), pp. 15–16.
10 Max Weber, *Essays in Sociology,* translated by H. H. Gerth and C. Wright
Mills (New York: Oxford University Press, 1958), p. 214.

tional goals, the groundwork is laid for dysfunction. These unanticipated consequences include alienation of highly trained professionals; undue emphasis on procedural matters and creation of a certain resistance to change; distortion of the professional-client relationship, with a resultant tendency to treat the public served in a formal, impersonal manner; development of a legalistic attitude toward the performance of official duties, avoidance of responsibility, and minimization of commitment to and involvement in the organizational endeavor; and the appearance of informal groups which attempt to influence policy within the organization. Traditionally, many of these dysfunctional elements have been viewed as direct outgrowths of the attempt to delineate authority and responsibility inherent in individual offices and to impersonalize relationships between members of the organization through a body of rules.[11]

### Bureaucratic Attributes of Schools

Because schools have inherited much of the classical tradition of organization and administration, they exhibit many bureaucratic characteristics. The strong, asymmetrical exercise of authority and control from top to bottom is one obvious expression of this tradition. In order to exercise control of potentially disruptive students, for example, schools have resorted to at least three widely used techniques:

1. The use of rules, often differentially applied.
2. Segregation of students into classes, tracks and schools.
3. Differential treatment in such matters as discipline, giving marks, and awarding symbols of status.

Similarly, efforts to control potentially disruptive teachers include:

1. The use of rules.
2. Differential treatment in the assignment of classes, facilities, schedules, and symbols of status.
3. Manipulating the system's rewards—both tangible and intangible.

However, alienation and resistance to the bureaucratic system can reach the point where the power of the hierarchy to control it is threatened. In a bureaucratic organization, as in any other organization, *superordinates are highly dependent upon their subordinates to achieve the desired goals.* Thus, teachers confronted with really disruptive students—students who care little about rules or the school's idea about status—tend to reduce the formal impersonality with their students. They tend, instead, to individualize instruction and the issuance of marks,

---

[11] James G. Anderson, *Bureaucracy in Education* (Baltimore: The Johns Hopkins Press, 1968), p. ix.

differentiate assignments, and seek new curricula and materials more suitable for their students. Indeed there is evidence that, on this basis, teachers of lower socioeconomic children try newer techniques and materials more readily than those who teach middle- or upper-class students.[12]

This debureaucratization on the part of teachers creates a dilemma for the administrator, however, as his role in the classic organizational concept is to apply the rules and procedures impartially and impersonally to all. In his bureaucratic role he is charged with the responsibility for executing the rules and policies of higher authority through supervision of those below him. On the other hand, the school is highly vulnerable to the opinions and actions of its students and the members of the community. The resultant pulling and hauling of countervailing interests and responsibilities usually results in either (1) an escalating conflict that the administrator rarely wins or (2) the adoption of a relatively personal style by the administrator in which he establishes personal relationships with parents, students, and teachers as a defense.

This debureaucratic adaptation may be contrasted with the organizational response to rising teacher militancy. Since the school is not nearly as vulnerable to teachers—even though they may strike—as to parents and community people, the response to their demands is characteristically bureaucratic. The hierarchy, in order to retain and exercise its power to control the teachers, may enforce rules with scrupulous care and promulgate new ones. Rules may also be sought from higher authority—such as new laws from the legislature and new interpretations from the courts. Great care is taken to reinforce formal impersonal relationships, emphasizing the letter of the negotiated contract, strict interpretation of grievance procedures, and punctilious observance of required role performance.

Of special concern to schools is the conflict between the authority relationships of bureaucratic hierarchical discipline on the one hand and the concepts of professionalism that teachers widely hold on the other hand. There are crucial differences between the bureaucrat and the professional:

1. the professional's first loyalty is to his profession and his clients' interests, whereas the bureaucrat's responsibility is to uphold the organization and its interests.
2. the professional's authority stems from his expertise and his conduct is governed by the standards and ethics of his discipline, whereas the bureaucrat's authority resides in the position he currently holds and he is controlled by rules and hierarchical discipline.

[12] Ibid., chapter V, "The Effects of Bureaucracy on the Schools."

3. the professional is judged by his colleagues and clients, whereas the bureaucrat is evaluated by his superordinates in the organization.

There is persistent conflict in the school between the concepts of *professional autonomy* and *bureaucratic authority*. In a real sense it is a conflict between the values of professional responsibility and self-determination against the values of bureaucratic rules and procedures. Many times, of course, highly trained and expert teachers are impatient with the restrictions of rules and formalized procedures that hamper their professional autonomy. Administrators, however, with an eye to total organizational coordination and performance are inclined to use rules to heighten their sense of control.

There is empirical evidence to support the common-sense view that the hierarchical authority structure generally found in schools and school systems and the manifestation of that authority through the equitable application of rules are not totally dysfunctional in schools.[13] Indeed, since the essence of organization is coordinated effort, the existence of well-defined policies, careful delineation of responsibilities, and clear-cut procedural rules appear to provide the participants with confidence that they know what to expect and how to deal with the organization. On the other hand, ambiguous job expectations, conflicting directives from superordinates, and uncertainty as to one's authority and responsibilities inhibit productive effort and increase unfavorable attitudes toward supervisors and administrators.

While bureaucratized schools and school systems may be faulted for their emphasis upon hierarchical authority exercised asymmetrically from the top down and the proliferation of formal rules as inhibitors to change, the argument is not all one-sided. In concept, at least, the clear delineation of authority and rules permits teachers to know how to influence school policy. In an ambiguously organized system, however, the lack of structure in itself makes teachers uncertain as to how to express their views effectively.

*The substitution of a relatively unstructured system for a bureaucratized system, then, is an inadequate administrative response to the need for greater flexibility in schools. Indeed, the low-structure situation may very well heighten the threat, anxiety, and powerlessness that the individual experiences, leaving him unsure as to how he may deal effectively with the system.*

13 See, for example, Arthur R. Cohen, "Situational Structure, Self Esteem, and Threat-Oriented Reactions to Power" in Dorwin Cartwright, ed., *Studies in Social Power* (Ann Arbor: Institute for Social Research, University of Michigan, 1959); also James G. Anderson, "Authority Conflict and Control in Schools," in *Bureaucracy in Education*.

### Distinctive Organizational Characteristics of Schools

Classical organization theorists seek to develop universal concepts of the organization and its management that can be applied to all organizations. These concepts are expressed in terms of principles that underlie organization and administration as a systematic field of practice. These include the familiar *scalar principle* (e.g., authority descends in an unbroken line down the hierarchy from the highest administrator to the lowest participant); *unity of command* (the concept of line and staff); *accountability* (the exercise of delegated responsibility in terms of established performance standards); and the *profit center concept* (each subunit of the organization is evaluated in terms of cost/effectiveness). The classical approach to administration tends to stress propositions as to what administrators should do as general principles of management.

A more contemporary approach to the comparative study of administration seeks (a) the characteristics generally shared by most types of organizations and (b) to identify the explicit characteristics of a specific organization under consideration. The latter approach seeks not so much methods that may be universally applicable as understanding the distinctive needs of specific organizations.

Schools possess a number of distinctive characteristics that distinguish them from other organizations [14] and have implications for the administration of change not universally found in all organizations.

1. *They are people-changing organizations.* More specifically their focus is on children-changing. This is a predominant characteristic of the school, of course, and the implications for sharing the change-induction with the family, church, and other social agencies are important aspects of dealing with this fact. This is a particularly sensitive issue, too, in that it involves dealing with ethics, mores, and belief systems of a disparate population.

2. *Involuntary membership.* Compulsory attendance laws plus the realities of the job market in a highly industrialized society fill the American schools with young people who may or may not choose to be there.

3. *Diffuse goals.* In our highly pluralistic society the "common school" is faced with the dilemma of numerous, often conflicting and overlapping, diffuse and ambiguous goals.

4. *Political control.* Because of the need to maintain a constituency with a strong plurality at all levels—local, state, and national—the school is vulnerable to the ebb and flow of political tides. Even though "local

---

[14] This discussion follows Matthew B. Miles, "Some Properties of Schools as Social Systems" in Goodwin Watson, ed., *Change in School Systems* (Washington, D.C.: National Training Laboratories, NEA, 1967).

control" remains a popular image, the actual political forces of control over schools are diffuse and difficult to identify clearly.

5. *Low internal interdependence.* Schools are generally (1) minimally staffed and (2) organized so that the teachers work apart from one another. Thus, there is very little opportunity to develop the kinds of on-the-job linkages that foster the ongoing interaction essential to the development of new ideas and creative problem solving. Similarly, schools within school districts and districts within regions tend to be isolated from one another, having few active communication links with one another. This is especially significant in terms of change; the opening up of communication for the free exchange of problems and ideas is an especially important element of organizational change.

6. *Professionalism.* Isolation from professional peers on the job, few career opportunities for individual growth and development, the generally "dead-end" nature of teaching as a career, are among the problems of teaching as an occupation. Coupled with this is the inability of teachers to wrest the full prerogatives of professionalism from public agencies in their quest for a greater voice in improving educational practice. The occupational immaturity enforced upon teachers as semi-professionals in a bureaucratic organization over which they have little control gives rise to motivational and morale problems that have strong influence over efforts to change the schools.

## SUMMARY

Administration has been defined as working with and through individuals and groups to accomplish organizational goals. Virtually until the middle of this century administration had been taught and learned as an art based upon the experience and shrewdness of older practitioners. Contemporary administration, however, is increasingly using approaches based upon the analysis of organizations utilizing behavioral science concepts and knowledge. Thus, the administrator is increasingly concerned about the application of appropriate knowledge and the concepts of organizational theory to problems of administering change in schools.

Change, as defined in this book, is a planned, systematic, controlled effort to alter more than one of the following aspects of the organization: (1) its tasks, (2) its structure, (3) its technology, or (4) its participants in ways thought to be more effective in achieving the organization's goals.

Administering change in schools, then, rests upon an analysis of the school as an organization. Until the present time the dominant analysis of organizations had been from the classical viewpoint, based upon bureaucratic concepts. Classical organizational theory seeks first and foremost a rational solution to organizational design and is primarily concerned with formal structure. The hierarchical pyramid of control—asymmetrical exercise of power and decision making authority from the top down, emphasis on clear written rules, and impersonal relationships —is basic to the classical organizational structure.

American schools have been heavily influenced by classical organization thought and generally reveal many bureaucratic attributes. While classical theorists tended to seek universal principles that would apply to all organizations, contemporary analysts also stress the need to assess the distinctive characteristics of a particular organization in order to understand it. Schools have a number of distinctive, if not unique, characteristics:

1. They are people changing organizations.
2. They have involuntary membership.
3. Their goals are diffuse and ambiguous.
4. They are responsive to political control.
5. They have low internal interdependence.
6. There is ongoing conflict between their semiprofessional participants and hierarchical organizational control.

## SUGGESTED READING

ANDERSON, JAMES G. *Bureaucracy in Education.* Baltimore: The Johns Hopkins Press, 1968. This volume by a research professor of educational administration is based not only upon the author's scholarly analysis of the subject but also upon a research study of a metropolitan school district.

BLAU, PETER M. *Bureaucracy in Modern Society.* New York: Random House, 1956. This authoritative and readable paperback classic by a noted sociologist is probably the most widely read book on the subject. It clearly relates bureaucracy to significant contemporary social problems.

DREEBEN, ROBERT. *The Nature of Teaching: Schools and the Work of Teachers.* Glenview, Illinois: Scott, Foresman and Company, 1970. This analysis goes beyond the usual claims to professionalism generally heard in schools and explores the occupational aspects of teaching and their organizational constraints. It suggests that the occupation can be enriched to the benefit of both teacher and school.

ETZIONI, AMITAI, ed. *The Semi-Professions and Their Organization.* New York: The Free Press, 1969. This is a sociological analysis of the conflict between administrative authority and the semiprofessions (such as nursing and public school teaching). Includes an excellent study of school problems.

MARROW, ALFRED J., BOWERS, DAVID G., and SEASHORE, STANLEY E. *Management by Participation.* New York: Harper and Row, 1967. Marrow was chairman of the board at The Harwood Manufacturing Company at the time of the Weldon takeover. He was also a behavioral scientist. While this book describes the application of behavioral science to the change problems of an industrial firm, the concepts and techniques used clearly have relevance to schools.

# CHAPTER 3

# educational administration
# and
# organizational change

Administrative thought on organizational change in schools has been characterized by the lack of a clear conceptual analysis. Popular among the approaches taken by educational administrators have been the following:

1. Change is likely when individuals with certain distinctive characteristics that mark them as "innovators" are placed in key positions in the organization.
2. Change results from the communication of knowledge about new discoveries and inventions from researchers to practitioners so that they may be implemented in the school.
3. Change in schools is positively related to financial support.
4. Change in schools is dependent upon in-service training designed to constantly improve the professional competence of teachers.
5. Change can be effected through meticulous close supervision of teachers designed to improve their skills on the job and to be sure that they follow correct instructional procedures.

## CHARACTERISTICS OF INNOVATORS

Extensive study of innovative people seems to confirm the popularly accepted view that, as a group, they do tend to possess certain characteristics. They are, for example, inclined to be among the younger members of their occupation or profession.[1] They tend, also, to be cosmopolitan; they travel, see other people in their profession, and usually think of themselves as professionals whose primary frame of reference is their clients and the profession at large rather than the specific organization.

Locally oriented individuals, on the other hand, tend to view the world more in terms of the place (the school or the community, for example) to which they are attached.[2] The cosmopolitan educational administrator attends a good many meetings, is active in regional or national groups, and is interested in studying the ways other people have solved problems. If an opportunity arose that meant professional advancement, he would probably leave his present job very readily, whereas the local might stay where he is for a variety of reasons.

Similarly, the innovator tends to be well-located in communication networks, both formal and informal: he knows many people, talks with others a great deal, and picks up new ideas earlier than others. The innovator wishes to change the status quo; he feels comfortable in exploring new ideas (even though he may discard them) and questions the established order of things. He tends, also, to advance in his career faster and earn more money than others.

Of course, these are generalizations that are difficult to apply to individuals in specific situations. For example, in employing a young person there is obviously no guarantee that he will be an innovator. But usually an individual who has a mix of these characteristics is more likely to be innovative than not.

However, an organization that is engrossed with the need to limit, regulate, and control its participants—such as a bureaucratic organization —is not likely to provide even highly innovative people with opportunities to perform in innovative ways after they are actually on the job. Indeed, the organization will strongly tend to mold the newly recruited participants in its own enduring image. *Therefore, while there is some research support for the common practice of recruiting younger people who are thought to be "open to change" as a means to stimulate change in schools, it will generally produce little result unless the organization develops processes whereby it will be responsive to their initiatives.*[3]

[1] Everett M. Rogers, "What Are Innovators Like?" in Richard O. Carlson et al., *Change Processes in the Public Schools* (Eugene, Ore.: The Center for the Advanced Study of Educational Administration, University of Oregon, 1965), pp. 58–59.

[2] The terms *local* and *cosmopolitan* are used here in the sense described by Alvin W. Gouldner in "Cosmopolitans and Locals: Toward an Analysis of Latent Social Roles," *Administrative Science Quarterly,* II (December, 1957; March, 1958), pp. 281–306 and 440–80.

[3] For a thoughtful discussion of this point based upon extensive research see Norman Frederiksen et al., *Prediction of Organizational Behavior* (New York: Pergamon Press, Inc., 1972), especially chapter 12.

School boards that are seeking a new superintendent of schools, one who will encourage change, are frequently advised by search consultants to seek a person from outside of the district, preferably one with cosmopolitan characteristics. On the other hand, boards that are looking for a school superintendent at a time when the board hopes for a period of stability are often advised to look for someone from within the system who appears to be local in his orientation and place-bound in his career. A compromise would be to seek a candidate who may be presently employed outside of the district but still reveals through his pattern of past activities that he is, essentially, local in his view of the world.

Educational administrators have long believed that low teacher turnover (or, conversely, a high retention rate of staff) is essential to the development of a high-quality educational program in schools. There is evidence from quality measurement studies in schools, however, that it is probably true only up to a certain point. Schools unaware of the significance of this can eventually find themselves with a highly stable staff—composed mostly of people with few characteristics of innovators. There are no places for younger, more cosmopolitan people, leaving a large percentage of the staff comprised of locally oriented people who are not inclined to see things change.

Thus, knowledge of the characteristics of innovators is important to the school district's personnel program for recruiting, selection, placement, and promotion practices in particular. Carefully-drawn job descriptions, unambiguous standards of performance criteria for teachers, and clear communication about the district's interest in having innovative and change-oriented people on its staff are some of the ways in which administrators can help to guard against stagnation and inbreeding that so often accompany efforts to achieve minimum staff turnover.

Genuinely innovative people usually respond best to opportunities to play a meaningful role in change and problem solving; characteristically, they will look for such opportunities wherever they may be found and do not feel especially committed to the organization in which they happen to be employed. Therefore, providing such opportunities is important in order to retain these people in the school. It is useful for administrators to know if the individuals who comprise their staff have the characteristics of innovators. However, since control over the composition of the staff—especially over a long period of time—is so limited, this approach cannot be considered a strategy for change in itself.

One can speculate, based upon commonplace observations such as these, that a school requires some measure of teacher turnover—some infusion of "new blood"—to keep the organization revitalized. In practical terms this is often evidenced—at both the university and in the public school—by efforts to reduce or eliminate teacher tenure: the belief being that the institution must suffer only so much "dead wood" on the faculty and must have ways of maintaining some optimum level of staff turnover. While it is obviously true that there must be protection against incompetent or otherwise inadequate individuals in the profession, it is also true that organizations have other options open to them to assure a growing and developing faculty. Our position is that in order to enhance the organization's capability for change, administrators need to develop ways of providing environments in schools that not only attract and hold innovative teachers but also that encourage the development of the entire staff to realize its highest professional potential.

## THE CONCEPT OF ADAPTABILITY

In exploring the differences between those school systems that might be called early adopters of change and those that are late adopters, Paul Mort sought to develop some sort of scalar dimension along which the relative standing of school systems could be identified. *Adaptability* was the concept used; the term referred to the extent to which the school system (1) responded effectively to its role in society and (2) adopted new operational techniques and inventions. Of course, it was felt that a high level of adaptability was a desirable characteristic of a school system. By investigating the components of that characteristic it was hoped that ways and means might be found to improve the adaptability of lagging school systems. In this way, perhaps, the nationwide lag in the diffusion of educational innovation could be reduced.

Measures of adaptability were developed, the best known of these being Mort's *The Growing Edge* that appeared in 1945.[4] One of the primary aims of the adaptability studies was to provide the local school administrator with comparative data on the impact of local policies and practices on the quality of education offered in the district's schools; the studies provided, in a sense, a measure of quality control that the administrator had not had before. Important dimensions of adaptability studies were:

1. *The community:* such factors as school-community relations, socioeconomic characteristics of the community.
2. *Administrative arrangements:* factors including class size and staffing patterns.
3. *Staff characteristics:* the age, training, background, turnover, etc., of the district's professional staff.

[4] Paul R. Mort, William S. Vincent, and C. A. Newell, *The Growing Edge* (New York: Metropolitan School Study Council, 1945).

4. *Expenditure analysis:* the adequacy and use of fiscal resources available to the school district (e.g., low teacher salaries v. high capital expenditures or high teacher salaries v. low capital expenditures).

An interesting facet of the adaptability studies is that instead of relying only on the gathering of data from questionnaires and existing reports, they generated increasing interest in what occurred between children and teachers. One way of assessing this in the classroom was through the training of people to observe and report classroom interactions using standardized reporting forms and procedures. This practice was advocated by Mort and his followers, as they tried to find ways to assess school quality that would be more accurate than the traditional, often discredited measures of quality (e.g., class size, rate of teacher turnover, cost per student).

This line of investigation, still continuing in the 1970s, led to the development of so-called *indicators of quality* that focused on four dimensions of in-classroom activity: (1) individualization, (2) interpersonal regard, (3) group activity, and (4) creativity. The indicators of quality observation guide that is used by trained observers consists of fifty-one items, each of which is scored by the observer on a plus-to-minus scale.[5] By 1970, 18,528 in-classroom observations from 9,961 elementary schools and 8,567 secondary schools had been recorded using this instrument in a nationwide group of school districts that were members of either the Associated Public School Systems, the Central School Study, or the Metropolitan School Study Council.[6] Correlated with data relating to the community, the administrative arrangements, staff characteristics, and financial situation of the school districts in which the observations were made, the research has yielded considerable insight into educational change as a diffusion process.

A number of conclusions have been drawn from this work, spanning over twenty-five years. Those of particular importance to us here are:

1. Innovations are adopted slowly in our schools, but according to a discernable pattern. Typically, it takes about fifty years for the need of innovation to be generally recognized. It takes an additional fifty years for the practice to be generally adopted (the diffusion period). During the fifty-year diffusion period, it takes about fifteen years for three percent of schools to adopt the change. That is followed by a twenty-year period of rapid popularization of the innovation, amidst much fanfare and publicity. After that, the practice is quietly adopted by most schools.

[5] *Indicators of Quality: A Brochure* (New York: Institute of Administrative Research, Teachers College, Columbia University, 1968).
[6] Martin N. Olson, "Classroom Variables That Predict School System Quality," *IAR Research Bulletin*, 2 (November, 1970): 1–8.

2. Characteristics of the community—especially its socioeconomic composition—have much to do with the degree to which the schools adopt change. This is directly related to such factors as (a) public understanding of what schools can do, (b) the citizens' feeling of need for education of their children, (c) their consequent views as to what teachers should be permitted to do and (d) the extent to which the public is willing to support the schools financially. Mort felt that this area—the shaping of the expectations and understandings of citizens so as to increase the level of financial support—was one of the most effective areas in which administrators could work to enhance the probability of support for change.

3. Educational innovators—including teachers and administrators—should be aware of how long it takes to diffuse change through the system. This knowledge would (a) help them through the inevitable discouraging periods of slow dissemination and (b) cause them to seriously question a change that was spreading at a remarkably slower rate than would normally be anticipated.

In practice, much of Mort's work was interpreted operationally as the "cost-quality relationship," which posited that per-pupil cost was the best single indicator of how much lag a school district would exhibit in adopting change. Under this influence, educational administrators exerted considerable effort to convince communities—and this included whole states as represented by state legislatures—as to the wisdom and need to provide increasing levels of tax-levy funds to school systems. Unfortunately, as the public financial support for schools rose through the period of the 1950s and 1960s, there was little widely accepted evidence that the high-expenditure school systems were in fact exhibiting the high level of adaptability that had been predicted for them. In addition, as the tempo of social change accelerated there was increasing reluctance to accept Mort's timetable for the diffusion of change in education as immutable and inevitable.

## EDUCATIONAL CHANGE IN THE POST-SPUTNIK ERA

Following the success of *Sputnik I* in 1957, a spectacular attempt to change the schools in fundamental ways was undertaken utilizing far different concepts from those previously accepted. Among these was the Physical Science Study Committee (PSSC) that sought, under the leadership of Professor J. R. Zacharias of the Massachusetts Institute of Technology, to overhaul and improve the teaching of physical science in American high schools (a) as speedily as possible and (b) with a relatively modest budget. Had the PSSC group accepted the existing views regarding change in the American public schools, they would have been well-pleased to see the job done in the conventional fifty years at an immeasurable overall cost. Instead, a decade after the project was launched a high school that had not adopted the PSSC program was considered to be behind the times.

### PSSC Strategy and Tactics of Change

The change strategy that the PSSC project employed was not developed as a grand scheme, mapped out in detail before the project was launched. It was developed and implemented by the project staff as practical problems presented themselves and had to be solved. In retrospect, however, it provides a model that is not only interesting and practical, but also one that has had considerable effect on the views of many educational reformers as to ways of bringing about widespread educational change rapidly.

The PSSC project was not an attempt to change the American schools in any broad sense; it was not an effort to "turn the schools around." The project started with the assumption that something was very wrong with the then-existing state of instruction in the physical sciences in American high schools. The general aim of PSSC was to try to correct the deficiency. With this limited, but hardly insignificant, target for change the project in effect developed a three-phase strategy: (1) to invent a new curriculum in the physical sciences for high schools, (2) spread knowledge of the newly-invented curriculum rapidly throughout the nation's high schools, and (3) facilitate its adoption in the schools. In general terms this was obviously a change effort based on the familiar diffusion strategy that Mort had studied so thoroughly. However, rather than "let nature take its course," the PSSC project developed and implemented some tactics that speeded up the diffusion and adoption process remarkably.

The first phase of the PSSC project, the invention of the new curriculum, was viewed as something to be done by scientists who were especially qualified because of their thorough knowledge of the structure of the physical science disciplines. Accordingly, a group of scientists was assembled along with a small staff to do the job. Thus, the new invention was created; but it would hardly be a change in the public schools until it had been adopted by them.

The second phase, diffusion of the invention to practitioners, would have been accomplished conventionally through such activities as the writing of books and articles, presentations at teachers conventions, and inclusion of it in college and university courses; and it could easily have taken fifty years (and possibly a century) to accomplish.

PSSC chose different tactics: (1) some forty institutes were established each year for the express purpose of providing the nation's high school physics teachers with intensive opportunities to study the new curriculum and learn how to use it, (2) relatively generous financial stipends and grants, that were easily obtained, were provided to encourage attendance at these institutes by as many teachers as possible. (The grants were not limited only to the teacher; married teachers could obtain additional funds to help defray the cost of bringing their families to the institutes, many of which were held in the summer. This undoubtedly increased the attractiveness of the institutes to those teachers who otherwise might not have attended).

The third phase of the PSSC strategy, adoption and implementation of the new curriculum, was also facilitated by the use of some novel tactics. One was the development of a complete curriculum "package" that included everything necessary to implement the new curriculum: films, tapes, teachers' guides and laboratory guides, textbooks, tests, and specifications for apparatus. Thus, the prospective adopter knew just what to use and how to use it without having to search around for ways to implement the ideas and trying to figure out how to deal with problems. This not only increased the likelihood that the curriculum would be adopted, but increased the probability that it would be fully and correctly implemented without debilitating changes being made at the local level. A second tactic that enhanced the implementation of the project was the provision of Federal funds that could be matched with local funds for the purchase of needed equipment and apparatus. This made it relatively easy to get the prompt cooperation of local school boards and administrators in meeting the initial costs of the new project.

The rapid appearance of the PSSC curriculum in the high schools across the country attested to the power of the new tactics to speed the diffusion strategy of change in schools. In effect, the PSSC experience may have contributed more through its contribution to our insight into change processes than the new curriculum which it set out to develop.

Other curriculum study groups have followed the lead of PSSC with variation on the strategy and tactics that it employed: the Biological Sciences Curriculum Study (BSCS), the Chemical Bond Approach Project (Chem Bond or CBA), and the School Mathematics Study Group (SMSG), are notable among them. By the 1960s, widespread disappointment with the apparent effect of educational changes that focused upon the limited concept of curriculum represented by these projects brought about a reduction in these kinds of efforts in favor of seeking more fundamental changes in the schools *as organizations*. The *strategy* and *tactics* used by many of them, however—such as Head Start—were remarkably similar to the PSSC experience.

## The Study of Educational Change in New York State

In a study of New York State, Henry M. Brickell analyzed the dynamics of educational innovation utilizing the discovery-diffusion-adoption sequence that Mort and his colleagues at Teachers College, Columbia University, had popularized.[7] His major observations may be summarized thus:

1. Though he found considerable instructional innovation in schools throughout the state, the schools that had adopted them were in themselves little changed *as organizations*. Changes usually consisted of such practices as new courses (e.g., "new" math, new courses in science), team teaching, or a changed class schedule in the high school with little fundamental impact on the school itself.
2. Many new ideas were being taken off the drawing board and installed in schools with little or no evaluation of their merits under conditions comparable to the public school situation.
3. The introduction of innovative programs depended largely upon administrators with their power to either block or adopt a new idea. Brickell found such concepts as "shared decision making" and "full staff involvement" to be largely euphemisms to cover the administrator's power to get the faculty to do as he wished. Teachers, on the other hand, generally have little ability (in terms of their power in the organization) to introduce significant change. They are typically left to deal with minor changes within courses or within single classrooms.
4. Most instructional changes are either adopted outright from another school or taken from some practice being used in another school. Few instructional changes are invented within a school system. In fact, the most popular and effective way of learning about a new idea is to visit a school similar to the home school where the new practice is already in use.

## Research and Development Centers

In the 1960s a variety of research, development, and dissemination agencies were developed nationally as a direct product of the Federal government's increasing involvement in efforts to improve public education. For example, Federal legislation (and funding) established a nationwide network of ten research and development centers and eleven regional education laboratories.

Originally the labs were conceived as being identified primarily with the geographic regions that they would serve while the research and development centers were organized to focus on specific fields within

---

[7] Henry M. Brickell, *Organizing New York State for Educational Change* (Albany, New York: State Education Department, 1961).

education—such as vocational education, learning, testing, and occupational education. In practice, however, each lab tended to develop a specialized field of inquiry with which it became especially concerned.

Perhaps the research and development center best known to educational administrators is the Center for Educational Policy and Management (CEPM) at the University of Oregon. The overall concern of CEPM is in the area of instructional change, and this has led to work in such areas as organizational change and the improvement of decision-making processes in education. CEPM has developed five programs that are related to each other: (1) control of instructional policy, (2) organizational implications of instructional change, (3) strategies for organizational change, (4) system planning, and (5) the development of instructional materials suitable for the dissemination of the knowledge that the other four programs have developed.

### Educational Resources Information Center

The Educational Resources Information Center (ERIC) is another example of the Federal effort to facilitate educational change in the 1960s. This nationwide network of twenty clearinghouses provides a system through which research results and other knowledge may be disseminated readily to people interested in further information.

Each of the clearinghouses focuses on a specific area of discipline: perhaps the one best known to educational administrators is the ERIC Clearinghouse on Educational Management, also at the University of Oregon. It facilitates the dissemination of information from a wide variety of sources nationwide. Its activities include the microfilming of reports, articles, and other documents; producing indexes and abstracts to facilitate the quick location of pertinent material; and the preparation of bibliographies, literature reviews, state-of-the-knowledge papers, and other papers that attempt to analyze, synthesize, and interpret research on various topics in the broad area of educational management.

Thus, ERIC seeks to do much more than the herculean task of facilitating the dissemination of the outpouring of literature on educational administration; it seeks to give out information in such a form that it can most readily be *used* in a practical way.

### National Institute of Education

The founding of the National Institute of Education in 1972 is a third example of the impetus given to the development of new knowledge in education and its dissemination to the practicing profession. The idea for such an agency was proposed by the President during the 1968 election campaign and reemphasized in the President's 1970 message on education to the Congress. The overall purpose of the proposed agency was to foster basic research and experimentation in education.

The thrust of this research in the area of educational administration had two major goals: (1) to learn how schools and school systems could build and maintain an organizational capacity for self-improvement, and (2) to provide information direct from this research to policy-makers and practitioners concerned with developing similar local capacities.

### The U.S. Office of Education Study

In 1972, B. Othanel Smith and Donald E. Orlosky reported the findings of a survey of seventy-five years of educational change that they had carried out for the United States Office of Education. In designing their study, they chose to view educational change as a diffusion process —much as Mort and Brickell had done. Smith and Orlosky treated educational *changes* as *things*. They spoke of "installing" change and identified educational changes as relatively specific and describable entities, such as the "look and say method," "core curriculum," and "sex education." Their view of "successful" changes were those that had been "installed" and had permeated the educational system. Changes that had achieved a lesser status were considered failures. They became much concerned, also, with whether or not the change had originated inside or outside the educational system.

Table 3-1 shows a number of changes that were identified by Smith and Orlosky, together with data regarding their (1) date of origin, (2) source (i.e., inside or outside of the public schools), (3) rating in terms of the degree of success or failure of the changes, (as judged by Orlosky and Smith) (4) the focus of each change, which could be on (a) instruction, (b) curriculum, or (c) organization and administration. By examining each of these changes, all of which emerged on the educational scene in America over a seventy-five year period of time, as individual case studies the researchers were able to derive a number of generalizations which are of interest to those seeking a guide to the development of strategies and tactics for organizational change in education.

Following are some of the major conclusions of the Orlosky and Smith Study:

1. It is easier to change curriculum or administration in a school than it is to change methods of instruction.
2. Curricular and instructional changes tend to originate within the school, not from some external source. Legislation and social pressure have little effect on this process, whereas the professional insight of teachers has considerable influence. This finding does not seem to

**Table 3-1.** *Changes listed alphabetically, showing date of origin, source, rating of success, and focus.*

| Change | Post 1950 [a] | Source [b] | Rating [c] | Focus [d] |
|---|---|---|---|---|
| Ability Grouping | | I | 3 | A |
| Activity Curriculum | | I | 2 | B |
| Adult Education | | EX | 4 | C |
| British Infant School | X | I | 3 | B |
| Carnegie Unit | | I | 4 | C |
| Community School | | I | 2 | B |
| Compensatory Education | X | EX | 3 | B |
| Compulsory Attendance | | EX | 4 | C |
| Conservation Education | | EX | 3 | B |
| Consolidation of Schools | | I | 4 | C |
| Core Curriculum | | I | 1 | B |
| Creative Education | X | I | 1 | B |
| Dalton Plan | | I | 1 | A |
| Desegregation | X | EX | 3 | C |
| Driver Education | | EX | 4 | B |
| Elective System | | I | 4 | B |
| Environmental Education | X | EX | 3 | B |
| Equalization Procedures | | I | 4 | C |
| Extra-class Activities | | I | 4 | B |
| Flexible Scheduling | X | I | 2 | C |
| Guidance | | I | 4 | A |
| Head Start | X | EX | 3 | C |
| Home Economics | | EX | 3 | B |
| Individually Prescribed Instruction | X | I | 3 | A |
| International Education | | I | 3 | B |
| Junior College | | I | 4 | C |
| Junior High School | | I | 4 | C |
| Kindergarten | | I | 4 | C |
| Linguistics | X | I | 3 | A |
| Look and Say Method | | I | 3 | A |
| Media & Technology | | I | 4 | A |
| Microteaching | X | I | 3 | A |
| Middle School | X | I | 3 | C |
| Mid-year Promotion | | I | 1 | C |
| New Leadership Roles | | I | 4 | C |
| Nongraded Schools | X | I | 3 | C |
| Nursery Schools | | EX | 3 | C |
| Open Classroom | X | I | 3 | A |
| Phonics Method | | I | 3 | A |
| Physical Education | | EX | 4 | B |
| Platoon System | | I | 1 | C |
| Programmed Instruction | | I | 3 | A |
| Project Method | | I | 2 | A |
| Safety Education | | I | 4 | B |
| School Psychologist | X | I | 3 | C |
| Self-contained Classroom | | I | 3 | C |

**Table 3–1.**   (*Cont'd*)

| | | | |
|---|---|---|---|
| Sensitivity Training | X | I | 2 | A |
| Sex Education | X | EX | 2 | B |
| Silent Reading | | I | 4 | A |
| Social Promotion | | I | 4 | C |
| Special Education | X | I | 4 | B |
| Store Front Schools | X | EX | 3 | C |
| Student Teaching | | I | 4 | A |
| Team Teaching | X | I | 2 | C |
| Testing Movement | | I | 4 | C |
| Tests & Measurements | | I | 4 | A |
| Thirty-School Experiment | | I | 1 | B |
| Unit Method | | I | 2 | B |
| Unit Plan | | I | 2 | A |
| Updating Curriculum Content | | I | 3 | B |
| Visiting Teacher | | I | 2 | A |
| Vocational & Technical Education | | EX | 4 | B |
| Winnetka Plan | | I | 1 | A |

SOURCE: Donald Orlosky and B. Othanel Smith, "Educational Change: Its Origins and Characteristics," *Phi Delta Kappan* LII, No. 7 (March 1972), pp. 412–13.

a X indicates change originated after 1950.

b I = change originated within education; EX = change originated outside education.

c 4 = has permeated the educational system; 3 = sufficiently present that instances of the change are obvious; 2 = not generally accepted but has had some influence; 1 = has not been implemented.

d A = instruction; B = curriculum; C = organization and administration.

concur with that of Brickell, who found teachers rather powerless in influencing the change process; nor does it fit with the experience of the educational research and development centers and learning laboratories. It surely does not reflect the experience of the post-Sputnik curriculum projects.

3. If the change requires extensive retraining of teachers (such as the introduction of team teaching) it is not likely to succeed.

4. Curricular changes that call for updating content or broadening an existing subject have a good chance for success, whereas those that require a major overhaul (such as adding new subjects or eliminating existing subjects) do not.

5. Curriculum change that receives wide social support is likely to succeed. Curriculum change that is subject to wide social opposition will probably fail.

6. Attempts to change the administrative structure of the schools in any significant way are likely to fail.

7. Changes that extend the school system (such as community college or preschool programs) are likely to succeed, whereas internal administrative modifications (such as flexible modular class scheduling) are less likely to do so.

8. Change in one school has little effect; a diffusion system is needed to spread it.

9. Broad support helps to spread the change. For example, in the case of compulsory education, broad legal, social, and educational support assures its success. It is not likely that educators alone could have secured adoption of the change.

10. Changes that require people in established positions to relinquish power are not likely to be implemented.

11. The less people have to learn in order to make the change operational, the more likely it is to succeed.

12. The more energy the change demands from the school staff, the less probable is its success. Thus, creative education—which requires enormous amounts of teacher time and effort to implement—is not as likely to succeed as some new "packaged" curriculum.

Having made these generalities, Smith and Orlosky went on to point out that each specific situation must be appraised with care in developing procedures for the successful installation of educational change.

## CHANGE IN EDUCATION
## AS KNOWLEDGE UTILIZATION

The central point of the foregoing discussion is that the problem of directing and controlling deliberate change efforts has, traditionally and conventionally, been viewed by educational administrators as essentially one of knowledge utilization. It is a logical, rational view that stresses the need to incorporate into educational practice new knowledge constantly being discovered or invented by basic researchers (as distinguished from applied researchers). There is a difference between the statistical conjurations of scientific research and the practical application of concepts that emerge from systematic study in actual classrooms full of school children. Indeed, the average teacher is not primarily concerned with the conceptualization of new ways to teach but rather with how to conduct the class on a daily basis.[8]

To facilitate the transmission and interpretation of new concepts from their source to the ultimate place where they will be used requires the existence of a strategy: the Research, Development, and Diffusion (R, D, & D) strategy of change.[9] This strategy seeks to link research to

[8] John Holt, *What Do I Do Monday?* (New York: E. P. Dutton, Inc., 1970).
[9] This change strategy has different names in the literature; other popular names used are Research and Development (R & D) strategy or model of change and the "agricultural model." The R, D, & D designation seems to be most descriptive of the strategy, however, and appears to be coming into wider use. For an extensive discussion of the literature, see Havelock's *Planning for Innovation* suggested in the readings for this chapter. Also see Egon G. Guba, "Development, Diffusion and Evaluation" in Eidell and Kitchell's *Knowledge Production and Utilization in Educational Administration*, listed in the readings.

practice. The linkage is not simple, however, as shown in Figure 3-1. It requires a sophisticated network of related but clearly differentiated steps to bring the change to the final adopter in a form that is readily usable in a practical situation. Any breakdown in the chain that links research to practice is an obstacle for the success of the strategy. Such a barrier can result from a number of often complex causes.

One obvious barrier in the R, D, & D strategy applied to education is the frequently encountered situation in which there is, in fact, no established and dependable transmission network to carry out each of the vital processes shown in Figure 3-1; parts of the process are at times left to chance. This has often placed schools in the difficult position of attempting to carry out several phases of the process on a low-budget "do it yourself" basis—often actually getting involved in conducting applied research and producing their own product packages (e.g., curriculum guides, textbooks and workbooks, films, etc.) for their own adoption and use.

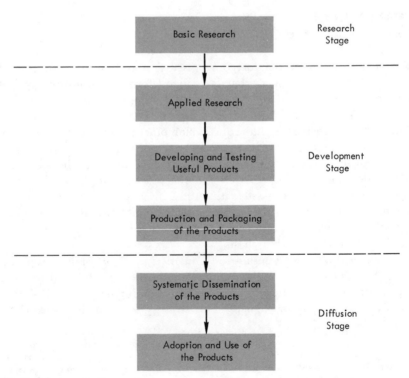

**Figure 3-1**
The Research, Development, and Diffusion concept of change strategy and tactics.

Another commonly encountered source of barriers in the R, D, & D process lies in the resistance to change often ascribed to the mores and social norms of human beings. The rational approach of the R, D, & D change strategy assumes that a rational individual will adopt the proposed change without resistance. In fact, this assumption is valid only if the change is proferred to the potential adopter in a way and at a time that is acceptable to him.

Since the administrator is primarily concerned about the diffusion stage of the R, D, & D strategy and his role in it, we shall concentrate on that stage.

*The diffusion process starts when the target client becomes aware that a solution to his problem has been invented or proposed.* In itself, this can be a complex process: the client, for instance, may not even know that he has a problem. A disadvantaged farmer eking out an existence in a poverty area may not have any idea that the pitiful rice crop he struggles to raise is far less than could be produced on his land. Similarly, a school teacher may not realize that the achievement of his pupils may be far less than they could do. The awareness stage of knowledge diffusion and utilization is very much subject to our perceptions of what is "real": our social values, our attitudes, how cosmopolitan we are, the characteristics of the system in which we work, the economic facts of life, and so on. In part, of course, this explains why many white, middle-class men and women who have become school teachers have had difficulty in understanding some of the problems they have found in teaching minority-group children.

Awareness can come about in other ways, of course. Court decisions are becoming increasingly important in making schools conscious of the need for change. New legislation, policy decisions by school boards, student protests, books—these represent a few of the many ways in which educators are made aware of problems. But awareness, as it is used in the knowledge utilization concept of change, has another significant dimension: that is the awareness that some knowledge or invention exists to deal more effectively with the problem at hand. Everyone who has dealt with the knowledge utilization problem in education has agreed on one point, at least: there is great need for a more effective network through which information regarding new inventions and new knowledge can be disseminated rapidly and clearly from the source to the ultimate adopters, so that the enormous traditional time-lag between invention or discovery and implementation in the schools will be reduced.

Much has been done to meet this need, especially beginning with the decade of the 1960s, through research and development centers, regional laboratories, the Educational Research Information System

(ERIC), and stepped-up efforts by state education departments. Publications, conferences for practitioners, intensive short in-service courses, participation in professional conventions and meetings, and use of such public media as newspapers and television have been used increasingly as aids in this effort.

*The second stage in the diffusion process begins when the potential adopter's interest is aroused.* If you know that some knowledge or invention exists but you feel it may not be useful to you, then you are not likely to become involved with it and (as far as you are concerned) the diffusion process is terminated. Or, on the other hand, if you know about something new but are unable to find out specific information about it, then you cannot seriously consider adopting it. Interest must be sustained and nourished by making it easy for the potential adopter to get further information about the proposed change.

The individual needs to gauge how practical the idea is in general. Are the costs of adopting the change likely to be within reason? Is his problem the same as the one that the new invention or process is designed to solve? Has it really produced the results indicated? If these questions can be answered affirmatively, the potential adopter is interested enough to further consider the merits of the proposed change and see if it is worth any more of his time.

*Evaluation is the next step in the diffusion process, in which the potential adopter studies the proposed change in some detail in terms of his specific situation.* He checks cost estimates. He tries to predict what problems the change will cause. He balances the proposed gains against the difficulties that will result.

*The fourth step in the diffusion process is to try it out on a small scale.* Few significant changes are adopted throughout the organization at this point. It is widely believed that segmental adoption is a better tactic because it meets with less resistance and it permits the inevitable adjustments to be made during the trial period, rather than later when the whole system is involved.

*Finally, the fifth stage of the diffusion process is adopting the change as standard practice and implementing it throughout the organization.* In education, especially, there is a high "washout" rate after adoption of change has apparently been achieved: a short time after adoption the change somehow disappears (usually quietly) from the scene. Change is often a fragile and delicate thing, and some provision for nurturing and supporting it at least for a period of time after its adoption can help it to survive over time. This can often be a monitoring and review system—such as a committee that has access to data about the on-going performance of the change—which provides the organization with feedback at appropriate decision-making levels.

## The Diffusion Process in Knowledge Utilization

The diffusion process, by which new knowledge moves from the source to practical application, has been studied widely. In a technological society, the linkages involved in diffusion seem to influence considerably the extent to which existing knowledge actually is applied in a rational and systematic way to solve social problems. The diffusion process has been studied in many contexts other than that of education. Its use by such diverse groups as villagers in agrarian societies, "detail" men of ethical drug houses, and managers in the Department of Defense has been studied. The effects of diffusion on individuals—even on vast organizations—has been assessed. From all this, considerable knowledge about the diffusion process itself has emerged.

### Elements in the Diffusion Process

There are four key elements involved in the diffusion process:

## 1. The nature of the change or innovation

Highly visible, readily describable, easily handled (e.g., neatly "packaged" in ready-to-use form, such as the PSSC curriculum) changes will be implemented more rapidly than vague changes subject to wide variations in interpretation.

  a. The relative advantage of the change, or the extent to which it appears more likely to achieve the school's goals or is more effective than present practice is important in determining the rate at which a change is adopted.
  b. Compatibility of the change with existing values is also important in determining the rate of adoption, as is knowing the past experience of the target of change.
  c. Divisible changes are usually more easily adopted, because they can be tried out in parts or stages over time. A change that must be fully adopted at one time or not at all tends to be adopted less frequently.
  d. Complexity also affects the diffusion rate. This need not be on a very sophisticated level: it is seen, for example, in the resistance of teachers to using motion picture projectors. Similarly, scheduling difficulties (as in the case of language laboratories) and the accessibility of needed equipment (e.g., the necessity of moving overhead projectors from room to room) can render a relatively simple change too complex for the average school.

## 2. Social-cultural factors in the diffusion process

Studies of change in the broad context of society have identified obvious social and cultural influences on the rate at which change is diffused and adopted. Farmers in southern India were asked how much land they would take if they were offered as much as they wanted as a gift. The overwhelming response was less than two acres: that was as much land as one man could till with a bullock in order to grow rice. It did not occur to them that, with more land, they could diversify their crops and employ labor-saving machinery; this simply had not been part of their experience. Schools, and education as a profession, also provide a social context with mores, values, and traditional expectations that have a great deal to do with the success or failure of efforts to introduce change. The following eight generalizations tend to facilitate rapid diffusion and adoption of a change:

a. Relatively little new behavior is required as most of the existing behavior may be retained.

b. The change is directed toward meeting needs that the participants in the organization already recognize and, preferably, have already tried to meet.

c. The change promises practical payoff in terms that are meaningful to the participants. This could be money, prestige, recognition, or satisfaction from achievement.

d. The change is introduced within the existing local power structure, utilizing local leadership, and respecting important local customs and traditions.

e. Those who are expected to implement the change are involved from beginning to the end, from planning through to evaluation: the participants have meaningful influence over important decisions in the process and are not merely engaged in peripheral matters.

f. Provision is made for a free flow of two-way communication between those responsible for managing the change and those expected to implement the change so that problems may be detected and considered quickly.

g. The managers of the change effort are flexible so that their tactics may be changed as needed to meet local conditions and unforeseen circumstances.

h. Provision is made for maintaining and supporting the change in the organization over time as it passes from the experimental stage to becoming part of regular operations. For example, it is difficult to prevent the washout of a change if the trial adoption was financed by external funding and final adoption of the change will require significant new outlays in the local expense budget in order to maintain it.

## 3. *Communication adequacy*

This is a third important element in the diffusion process. A society needs to have adequate systems for the spread of knowledge and ideas. In primitive societies this may involve such fundamental processes as developing literacy so as to facilitate the spread of technological ideas. In others communication is established through publications, meetings, and in-service courses. Individuals who are part of one system in society but are also connected with other systems provide valuable linkages of communication. For example, a study of the spread of "modern math" among the school districts of one state showed that the school systems that adopted the change earliest and most thoroughly had superintendents who communicated frequently with other superintendents by attending meetings where they picked up new ideas. Schools should encourage their staff to attend meetings away from home, to participate in professional groups, and to keep in contact with colleagues in other places so as to continue to exchange ideas.

## 4. *Time*

The element of time is also important in the diffusion process. Despite contemporary emphasis on increasing the tempo of change, it is essential in schools that adequate time be allowed for the change processes to occur: the decision-making, the development of psychological "readiness," the processes of trying to change, and evaluating the data which are gathered during the trial period.

It is difficult to estimate how much time is appropriate in a given change situation. While taking too much time obviously does not help, moving too swiftly can produce added strains and stresses that inhibit the success of a change effort. The 1972 decision by the Office of Economic Opportunity to terminate its sponsorship of experimental efforts in performance contracting after three years of effort was, for example, viewed by many as untimely. A change effort of such magnitude might well profit from formative evaluation feedback at that point in time but might require a longer period of nurturance before an ultimate evaluation could be undertaken.

## LIMITING FACTORS IN TREATING EDUCATIONAL CHANGE AS KNOWLEDGE UTILIZATION

The apparent effectiveness of knowledge utilization concepts in facilitating change in a number of fields—notably agriculture, medicine, science and other technological fields—has spurred many to advocate taking steps to develop applications of the process to education. This has been the thrust of many Federally funded attempts to aid in the improvement of American public schooling, such as the establishment of research and development centers, the support and sponsorship of various communication means such as publications and conferences, support and encouragement of a wide variety of research, and funding schemes aimed at facilitating the installation of changes in schools. The traditionally remarkable and unacceptable lag in adopting change in education might well be reduced by creating the machinery to facilitate diffusion of knowledge in education—such as the Research and Development model. Some of the problems that complicate applying the R & D model to education are:

1. Typically, in agriculture for example, the R & D model of change usually deals with an individual adopter, such as a farmer. In education, however, the adopter is an organization: a school or a school system. The problems of decision-making, resistance, and the whole process of adoption are enormously complicated by the fact that a complex group of people is involved.

2. The R, D, & D approach has been most successful in fields based upon the physical sciences, that provide a relatively precise, often exact, knowledge base from which to work. Education, however, is based largely on the social and behavioral sciences. While it is readily acknowledged that these sciences have been maturing with great speed, there are still many knowledge gaps that have to be filled in. Much of education is of an intangible nature, unlike the physical sciences. For example, a farmer can determine the advantage of planting a new variety of seed in his fields by comparing the bushels-per-acre produced using the new seed with what he would have gotten otherwise. Or, he can figure out whether he made more money when planting the new seed than he had previously. In education, however, the complex variables involved in determining what children learn make it difficult, when one tries a new idea, to assess with any precision what the effects of some new procedure actually are. The more we move away from the traditional notions of subject-matter to be memorized and begin to emphasize the affective aspects of school experience, the more difficult this problem becomes.

3. The change agent mechanisms so familiar in such technologically related fields as medicine and agriculture have not been well developed in education. A Federally assisted program has established eight research and development centers, each of which is charged with responsibility to (1) foster research, (2) encourage the development of procedures and products arising from this research so that they can be useful to schools, and (3) disseminate knowledge concerning these developments. Disregarding the fact that the number of R & D centers is pathetically limited when compared with the need, an important link in the diffusion chain has never been well developed in education: that is, some equiva-

lent to the Agricultural Extension Service to which schools and school districts could turn for practical help in dealing with change.

4. There is little incentive for schools to change. Unlike profit-oriented organizations, schools generally do not need to change in order to be assured of having enough money to continue operating; generally, no matter how well or how poorly schools are doing their job, they are protected by law from the equivalent of bankruptcy. Numerous suggestions have been made to make the schools more responsible so that their survival would depend upon their ability to meet certain reform measures. One of these suggestions has been the so-called "voucher plan," whereby parents could exercise consumer choice in educating their children; presumably, schools that lagged too badly in meeting the educational needs of their students would be hard-put to stay in business.

5. Educational goals are not clearly set forth. Assessing organizational performance of schools is rendered difficult because there is wide disagreement on just what those goals are or should be, and because in many cases the goals (particularly those dealing with the socialization of students) are stated in broad, general terms. This can be contrasted with the fundamental goal of a profit-making organization, when, for example, in the end, performance can be measured on the bottom line of a balance sheet. Numerous attempts have been made over the years to state, restate, and sharpen the goals of American education; but they continue to be as much a source of debate as agreement. In recent years there have been efforts to introduce precise instructional objectives stated in terms of the behavioral outcomes sought in the educational processes.

6. The professional preparation of teachers, and the semiprofessional conditions under which they work have not developed their abilities to develop and install change. Teacher training, long criticized for emphasizing classroom procedures and methods at the expense of developing scientific or humanities competencies, has tended to make teachers dependent upon others for inventing and evaluating new procedures; the tradition of close supervision and hierarchical authority in the school has further stifled efforts of teachers to develop changes on their own initiative.

7. There is no adequate evaluation and feedback as to the performance of the school or the teacher. The diffuse and multiple nature of the school's goals hamper efforts to evaluate its performance because there is confusion as to which goals are the important ones and those in turn are stated in too general terms. Recent efforts to develop more precise performance criteria based on behaviorally-stated goals should make it possible to (a) evaluate the performance of teachers and of schools more precisely and (b) relate various performance measures more directly to the instructional programs and procedures being used.

8. The schools are very vulnerable, being in the center of powerful social and political pulling and hauling. This kind of environment predictably produces cautious and conservative organizations rather than organizations willing to take risks. Change, as we have seen, requires full communication and creative partnership between the adopter and other agencies. Mutual striving toward common objectives is not enhanced by serious conditions of threat and conflict.

9. The funding of schools for operations is generally minimal, and little is available to try something new above and beyond existing practice. It has frequently been observed that schools put remarkably little into research and development that might lead to change; at the local level, such budget items are commonly attacked as unnecessary. This results, in part, in having an almost entirely operational staff with no one charged with the responsibility for developing new ideas, let alone handling problems of adopting change. It also results in public schools having virtually no risk capital or discretionary funds available that may be used to exploit an unexpected opportunity to initiate or nurture a change-oriented effort.

## SUMMARY

Educational administrators traditionally have tended to take a rather eclectic view of organizational change, relying upon a number of diverse views instead of a systematic analysis of the problem. Some of these views—such as the characteristics of innovators and the knowledge utilization point of view—are more helpful in understanding how individuals deal with change rather than understanding problems of organizational change. Administrators often feel uncertain as to how to encourage and facilitate planned organizational change systematically, because of the difficulties they experience in trying to utilize concepts in the management of organizational change that apply to individuals.

Since the 1960s, with increased leadership from the national level, much has been done to stimulate research, development, and knowledge diffusion applicable to education. A central goal of the United States Office of Education and other major agencies in the post-Sputnik period was to develop the knowledge base for teaching. The belief appears to have been that the resultant knowledge and techniques would be diffused in a manner not unlike the agricultural model. The concept was known as R, D, & D. The primary target of this massive effort was the teacher in the classroom.

While we have identified a number of factors that limit or inhibit the effectiveness of the R, D, & D approach in education, none is more central than the fact that the target of change is not the individual teacher alone but rather the school as an organization.[10]

Educational administrators—seeking ways to *manage planned organizational change*—must be concerned about the crucial internal processes of the organization that enable it *as an organization* to develop more effective ways of deciding what to do and how to do it. The contemporary administrator, therefore, must base his approach on a systematic analysis of organizational realities.

Conventional in-service education and close supervision not only tend to ignore recently understood organizational realities concerning schools, but also unwittingly aggravate the situation by emphasizing the low-status, dependent role of the teacher in the hierarchically oriented school setting. It is increasingly evident that the traditional situation in schools does little to motivate faculty members to involve themselves in their work at more than minimal levels. Planned organizational change intends to increase the effectiveness of schools in achieving their goals; it requires, however, increased interest, involvement, and energies of teachers in the total change process. Because the coercive power of administrators over teachers is—in this era of negotiations and rising egalitarianism—on the decline, new forms of administrative leadership are necessary. This new leadership—the kind required for participative management—requires knowledges, skills, and awareness of (a) the nature of organizations and (b) the processes of organizational change markedly different from those of the past.

## SUGGESTED READING

EIDELL, TERRY L., and KITCHELL, JOANNE M., eds. *Knowledge Production and Utilization in Educational Administration.* Portland, Oregon: University Council on Educational Administration and Center for Advanced Study of Educational Administration, 1968. Describes research, development, and diffusion in American public schooling.

HAVELOCK, RONALD G., in collaboration with Guskin, Alan. *Planning for Innovation Through the Dissemination and Utilization of Knowledge.* Ann Arbor: Center for Research on the Utilization of Scientific Knowledge, Institute for Social Research, The University of Michigan, 1969. This massive volume provides a comprehensive summary and description of

---

[10] This is vividly described in a study of two matched elementary schools whose pupils evidenced remarkably different reading achievement. The critical factors that differentiated the two schools appeared to be organizational climate and the leader behavior of the principal rather than such factors as class size, teacher skill, or instructional materials selected for use. See *School Factors Influencing Reading Achievement: A Case Study of Two Inner City Schools* (Albany, N.Y.: Office of Education Performance Review, State of New York, 1974).

the framework that underlies contemporary concepts of knowledge dissemination and utilization. The task is approached from four levels: (1) the individual, (2) the interpersonal, (3) the organization, and (4) the social system of society in general. This scholarly reference work with its extensive bibliography should be available to the educational administrator seriously interested in the broad field of change processes.

ROGERS, EVERETT M. *Diffusion of Innovations.* New York: The Free Press of Glencoe, 1962. Describes the processes of knowledge diffusion and utilization in society. Draws upon cases from a number of fields and various settings to illustrate the fundamental concepts. A highly readable book.

————. "What are Innovators Like?" In Richard O. Carlson, et al., *Change Processes in the Public Schools.* Eugene, Oregon: The Center for the Advanced Study of Educational Administration, 1965. A succinct summary of the state of knowledge regarding the characteristics of innovators.

# CHAPTER 4

# crucial factors
# in
# organizational change

Administering change in an organization requires efficiency. This does not mean, however, that in adopting a systemic approach an administrator can disregard human considerations. Demands for better organizational performance under contemporary conditions of rapid change *have* placed great emphasis upon efficiency. The administrator and the organization, beset by demands for humanizing the organization—emphasizing the need for greater human dignity, feelings of satisfaction, and even self-actualization—face what at times appears to be an antithetical force that tends to block rational management.

In the Hegelian construct we have a thesis: that rational, systematic, highly coordinated management systems are needed to give managers the tools needed for the planning, organizing, and controlling required of contemporary organizations. This suggests the implementation of such management systems as Planning, Programming, and Budget Systems (PPBS), Program Evaluation and Review Technique (PERT), and Management by Objectives (MBO). In the popular mind these are often accompanied by computer printouts, reorganization, work changes, new jargon (such as *cost-effectiveness* and *performance criteria*), and powerful centralized management control from distant and inscrutable sources.

To continue in Hegelian terms, however, we have an antithesis: one must consider the rising value on human dignity, the importance of the individual, and the rising insistence upon increased self-actualization (or, at least, a sense of purpose and self-worth). To many, this tendency suggests that workers in an organization ought to be more involved in decisions and in setting goals, and they ought to enjoy more latitude in their jobs.

A new synthesis (in the Hegelian sense) of thought and action in management has emerged from the clash between those who were primarily concerned with efficiency in an organization, versus those who were more humanistically oriented. This new synthesis utilizes a total systems approach to identify and describe the essential dimensions of organizational change. Harold Leavitt, using such an approach, has identified four dimensions of organizational change that may be used with flexibility in developing various change strategies for organizations.

## DIMENSIONS OF ORGANIZATIONAL CHANGE

By definition, an organization exists for the purpose of achieving something: reaching some goal or set of goals, by accomplishing certain *tasks*. Rationally, of course, the organization is structured, equipped, and staffed appropriately to accomplish its mission. The main goal of a business firm, for example is to make profits for its enterpreneurs and investors. In order to achieve such a goal, the firm must perform certain tasks: it must manufacture and sell products, or buy and sell products, or provide certain services.

In order to achieve an assigned task—that may include a large number of subtasks and operationally necessary tasks—we build an organization: that is, we give it *structure*. It is the structure that gives an organization order, system, and many of its distinctive characteristics. The structure establishes a pattern of authority and collegiality, thus defining role: there are top-management executives and middle-management supervisors, bosses and workers, each of whom attempts to know the extent of his or her own legitimate authority as well as that of others. Structure dictates, in large measure, the patterns of communication networks that are basic to information flow and, therefore, decision-making. Structure also determines the system of work flow that is, presumably, focused on achieving the organization's tasks.

The organization must have *technological resources* or, in other words, the tools of its trade. Technology, used in this sense, does not only include such typical hardware items as computers, milling machines, textbooks and chalk, and electron microscopes. Technology may also include program inventions: systematic procedures, the sequencing of activities, or other procedural inventions designed to solve problems that stand in the way of organizational task achievement.

Finally, of course, the organization must have *people*. Their contribution to the task-achievement of the organization is ultimately visible in their acts—that is, their organizational behavior. It is this behavior that selects, directs, communicates, and decides.

These four factors—*task, structure, technology,* and *people*[1]—are variables that differ from time to time and from one organization to the next. Within a given organization these four factors are highly interactive, each tending to shape and mold the others. They can be considered the key elements to be dealt with in attempting to change the organization. As in any system, the interdependence of the variable factors means

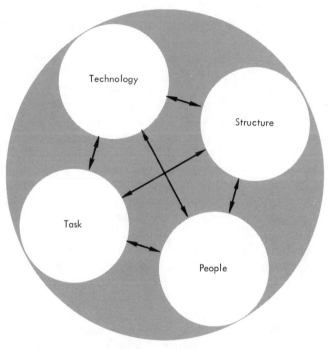

**Figure 4-1**
Interacting change variables in complex organization. Adapted from Harold J. Leavitt, "'Applied Organizational Change in Industry: Structural, Technological and Humanistic Approaches," in James G. March, ed., *Handbook of Organizations* © 1965 by Rand McNally College Publishing Company, Chicago, Figure 1, p. 1145.

[1] This view of organizational change is based upon the concepts developed by Harold J. Leavitt in *Managerial Psychology,* 2nd ed. (Chicago: The University of Chicago Press, 1964). *See also* by the same author, "Applied Organizational Change in Industry: Structural, Technological, and Humanistic Approaches," in James G. March, ed., *Handbook of Organizations* (Chicago, Ill.: Rand McNally & Company, 1965), pp. 1144–70.

that a significant change in one will result in some adaptation on the part of other factors. *This is the key to selecting strategies and tactics for organizational change.*

Suppose, for example, we have an academically oriented high school that admits limited numbers of talented students by competitive examination for the express purpose of preparing them for college. If the board of education rules that the school be converted into a comprehensive high school to meet the needs of the total youth population (which, of course, would be a change in the organization's task), it is apparent that a number of internal adjustments would be necessary for the school to achieve its new goal reasonably well. Many of these changes would be compensatory in nature. For example, in order to accommodate those students interested in a business career, business education equipment would have to be installed (technological), business education teachers would have to be employed (people), and a department of business education might be created (structural). However, some of the changes flowing from the board's directive might be retaliatory rather than compensatory. For example, some people in the school might seek to resist these changes, with the result that their former cooperative, productive behavior would be replaced by alienation and conflict. This, in turn, could disrupt the normal communications patterns in the school, thereby producing a structural change.

Another example would be the effects of a decision by the board of education to decentralize the operations of the school district, which would be a structural change. This could, quite possibly, result in some modification of the educational goals (task) of schools. It would probably produce at least limited technological changes, such as new record-keeping systems and purchasing procedures. Finally, decentralization would change the attitudes, sense of involvement, and motivation of people, including teachers.

A technological change, such as the introduction of a comprehensive computer-related instructional system in a high school, could bring about important side effects: it could change the goals of the school by making it possible to achieve new things and, simultaneously, render certain traditional tasks obsolete. A change in people would include the employment of new personnel with technical skills, affecting the work activities of others in the school by making some activities unnecessary and requiring certain new activities to be introduced. Finally, the introduction of new departments and changes in those involved in the decision-making processes would be structural changes flowing out of the technical change originally initiated.

Thus, in selecting a strategy for bringing about organizational change, we have options in choosing the primary target—people, structure, technology, or task. However, if we propose to introduce a significant change through primarily one of the target variables, it is clear that the other variables will soon be affected. Change efforts that are basically technological in nature result in some compensatory or retaliatory behavior on the part of people and some structural adjustments within the organization. Those who seek to bring about significant structural rearrangements in the school—such as differentiated staffing plans—must reckon with the people involved and the way they will react to the change.

While it is easy for us to speak of different change strategies and to categorize various tactics and procedures as "belonging" to one strategy or another, we must recognize the symbiotic interrelationship which exists among the variables with which we are concerned. So, while we deal here with four different organizational change variables—task, technological, structural, and behavioral—the differences between change strategies involve (a) the variable that is selected as the primary target within the organization and (b) the values that dictate the priorities in determining what *ought* to be done. In using a given strategy we are especially concerned with a particular organizational variable, but certainly not to the exclusion of the others.

## BEHAVIORAL SCIENCE VIEWS

Taxonomic inquiry is fundamental to the development of a scientific discipline. Some of the most promising efforts to describe and classify the options available to the administrator in selecting approaches to organizational change have been developed by behavioral scientists. Such inquiry identifies coherent strategies and tactics of change to replace the *ad hoc* tradition that has so often failed to meet the demands for change in the schools. Behavioral science analyses of organizations emphasize (1) the interdependent, collective nature of the subsystems of the organization while focusing on the dynamic, complementary interplay among them and (2) the dynamic interrelationship between the organizational system and its larger environment. Katz and Kahn believe that a common error in dealing with problems of organizational change is to forget the systemic nature of the organization and confuse individual change with changes in organizational functioning.[2] Thus, a member of the organization may be sent out to be trained in human relations expecting to utilize his new knowledge upon his return. But once the individual is again enmeshed in the ongoing social system—back in his old role—he is

[2] Daniel Katz and Robert L. Kahn, *The Social Psychology of Organizations* (New York: John Wiley & Sons, Inc., 1966).

locked into the same stresses and strains within the organizational system. Although his training may have been helpful to him as an individual, it has little effect upon the organization. Katz and Kahn emphasize the need for a systemic approach to organizational change with this observation:

> Some psychoanalysts . . . assume that wars are caused by the aggressive impulses of man and that if we can lessen frustrations and redirect aggressive impulses, we can change the belligerent character of the state and eliminate war. Reasonable as this sounds, it has very little to do with the case. The finger that presses the button unleashing a nuclear warhead may be that of a person with very little repressed hostilty, and the cabinet or state directorate behind the action may be made up of people who are kind to their families, considerate of their friends, and completely lacking in the psychopathology of aggression. They are merely carrying out their roles in a social system, and unless these roles and the social structure which gives them definition are changed, we will still have wars. Yet we persist in attempting to change organizations by working on individuals without redefining their roles in the system, without changing the sanctions of the system, and without changing the expectations of other role incumbents in the organization about appropriate role behavior.[3]

The analogy applies to schools. The escalating criticism of public schools in recent years has often included proposals to root out the supposedly inept or outright counterproductive professionals and thereby "turn the schools around." One writer, for example, devotes an entire chapter to "Firing the Staff" (including such topics as "How to get rid of a truly terrible principal").[4]

On another level, some political scientists feel that urban schools could be significantly changed by breaking up the big bureaucracies and decentralizing the political control of the schools through smaller community-oriented school districts. This approach seeks to heighten the vulnerability of the school to its environment. It is at least partially predicated on the belief that the members of the school's bureaucratic "establishment" tend to defeat efforts at change and need to be replaced. The assumptions underlying such approaches are that (1) the individuals who now occupy administrative roles in the schools are "bad" (e.g., stupid, lazy, bigoted, evil, ignorant), (2) that if they are replaced with people who are "good" (e.g. have the "right" attitudes and have a desire to make the schools better) then (3) the schools will begin to change for the better.

The appointment of a new administrator rarely results in significant

---

[3] *Ibid.*, p. 391.
[4] Ellen Lurie, *How to Change the Schools: a Parents' Action Handbook on How to Fight the System* (New York: Vintage Book, 1970).

sustained organizational change in the schools. Usually some change occurs shortly after the appointment of the new administrator [5] and then the organizational system finds a new homeostatic equilibrium.

Contemporary open social system concepts of the school as an organization posit that the primary target of organizational change efforts must be the *system,* the social structure that defines and describes the organization. This is the basis for selecting a change strategy. When we add a new individual to the system (or when we take an existing person out, retrain him, and place him back into the organizational system) it is highly unlikely that he can alter significantly the norms of peer groups, change the interpersonal relationships between people and groups, or otherwise redirect the behavioral norms and expectations in the organizational system. Indeed, that individual soon becomes a functional part of the existing social system—necessarily accepting and acting upon the expectations and norms of the organization. He cannot remain an outsider forever, holding different values and ideas than his coworkers and colleagues and expect to be very influential in redirecting the organizational system.

## TAXONOMIES OF CHANGE STRATEGIES

The vast literature on organizational change includes numerous attempts to identify and classify the many possible ways of changing organizations. Three of these, that will be discussed briefly here, have proven to be especially useful to researchers and practitioners alike. While each of the three approaches professes to be distinctive, the typology of task, structure, people, and technology is clearly implied in each of them.

The three taxonomies to be discussed here are the work of (1) Daniel Katz and Robert L. Kahn, (2) Ronald G. Havelock, and (3) Robert Chin and Kenneth D. Benne.

### *The Katz and Kahn Social System Approach*

Katz and Kahn have identified seven methods or strategies for bringing about organizational change: [6]

### *1. Information*

Giving information is the most traditional method of organizational change. When coupled with other change strategies that motivate people

---

[5] This is likely if the new appointee is from outside the system, less likely if he is selected within the system.

[6] Katz and Kahn, *The Social Psychology of Organizations,* Chapter XIII.

to want to adopt new ways, information becomes indispensable. A weakness of the information strategy for organizational change is that its target is generally the individual, and not the organizational system.

## 2. *Individual counseling and therapy*

This method may have advantages for the individual—perhaps by helping him realize his potential and giving him a sense of direction—but it is not focused on the organizational system as a target of change. Indeed, it can be dysfunctional: one thinks of the stereotype of the person who returns to work after a couple of weeks of sensitivity training only to find that he must once again readjust to the acceptable norms of the organization.

## 3. *Influence of the peer group*

It has been repeatedly shown that workers who are encouraged to discuss the problem and participate in important decisions as to what should be done adopt change more quickly, more thoroughly, and retain it longer than those who are simply told what to do. The processes of discussion and decision-making help to develop group cohesiveness and spirit, greatly influencing the behavior of the organization's participants.

However, merely to attempt to involve organizational participants in the decision-making process is not sufficient for success: there are a number of subtle factors that affect the outcome of peer-group involvement as a strategy for organizational change. For example, group discussion alone appears to have little effect on the group's acceptance of change; although the self-expression that such an opportunity affords may have a tonic effect, the group's norms and standards will hardly be affected unless the members are involved in making decisions and committed to carrying those decisions out.

But decision-making is not enough, either; the decisions, in order to have real effect on group functioning and standards, must be important *to the members of the group as a whole*. The decision—in order to be effective in shaping group norms—must be an *action* decision, something to which the group commits itself and in which it is involved. This strategy for change involves work groups and is not to be confused with representative groups—such as district-wide committees in which members represent constituencies; its essence is not representative involvement in the political bargaining processes by which broad decisions are reached, but rather direct involvement of peers in a work group mutually solving problems through group process.

This idea contrasts markedly with the traditional hierarchical concepts of classical management that view the lower participants in the organization as the passive instruments of management decision.

## 4. Sensitivity training

Essentially, the target of sensitivity training is the individual and not the organization; this is perhaps its greatest weakness as a strategy of organizational change. However, in recent years as a result of intensive experimentation, the application of sensitivity training to organizational groups has increased rapidly. Behavioral scientists who see this strategy as having great potential in redressing problems of personal, interpersonal, and group dimensions within bureaucracies have made considerable progress in adapting the laboratory method of education to such problems. Serious efforts to apply the sensitivity training strategy to problems of organizational change in schools are still sporadic today, though rapidly increasing in number and sophistication.

## 5. Group therapy within organizations

The Tavistock Institute [7] pioneered an organizational change strategy in British industrial firms that is founded on many elements common to sensitivity training approach, especially in its recognition of conflict between individual motives and organizational needs and the consequences of that conflict in terms of resistance to change. Basically, the strategy is to apply the principles of individual therapy to groups in the organizational environment.

Unlike the NTL-sensitivity training approach (that seeks to take individuals from their regular organizational environment to a cultural island retreat where laboratory learning can be undertaken), the Tavistock approach seeks to: (1) assist organizational groups that already feel a need for help to achieve some objective to which the group members feel committed and (2) apply the principles of therapy directly within the work setting, at all levels of the organization—and, thus, change the organization itself.

This approach emphasizes the view that the organization is a sociotechnical system, as distinct from being a social system unrelated to the constraints imposed by its "tools of the trade."

## 6. Data feedback

All organizations—being open social systems—receive feedback data on their operations. Not all organizations, however, make as much effort as they could to (a) receive as much feedback information as they might,

---

[7] The Tavistock Institute is a British organization devoted to the application of behavioral science to organizations and human affairs. Its counterpart in the United States is the National Training Laboratories.

(b) communicate the information to appropriate members of the organization, or (c) use it to improve the adaptability of the organization to changing conditions in its environment. Improving the organization's use of feedback on its functioning can lead to basic changes in the organization.

Essentially, there are two kinds of feedback data that are involved in organizational change: (1) one that gives information about the output of the system (i.e., *summative* data) and (2) one that gives information about the internal functioning of the system (i.e., *formative* data). In the case of schools, reading test scores and the number of awards received by students are summative data; absenteeism, classcuts, and other information reflecting the organizational climate of the school are formative data.

## 7. Systemic change

Katz and Kahn consider this to be the most powerful approach to changing human organizations because it focuses on the larger organizational system itself, rather than on intermediary changes in individuals or groups. The strategy calls for direct manipulation of significant organizational variables. Katz and Kahn give a detailed description of one experimental application of the strategy in a business firm, in which the central thrust of the change was to redistribute decision-making power in the organization so as to allocate more authority for making decisions at lower levels in the hierarchy.[8] When accomplished and put into operation this strategy was obviously an alteration of the very characteristics and structure of the basic organizational system. For that reason, many writers consider such an approach to organizational change as a structural change strategy (rather than a systemic change, a term used by Katz and Kahn). A structuralist approach to organizational change emphasizes inducing changes in the organizational behavior of participants by rearranging the organizational structure.[9] Such a view is based upon a systems frame of reference to conceptualize the interaction between the individual and the organization during organizational change.

A typical illustration of systemic change strategy applied to public schools is the reorganization of school districts. For example, the movement to decentralize large urban school districts—that became so popular in the urban crises of the late 1960s—was aimed at improving the human condition in the schools. As one study observed, ". . . the fundamental

[8] Their illustration is drawn from Nancy Morse and E. Reimer, "The Experimental Change of a Major Organizational Variable," *Journal of Abnormal and Social Psychology,* 52, 120–29.
[9] Keeping in mind that organizational structure is not defined by physical structures—such as walls and membranes—but is characterized by the behaviors of participants repeated over time so that a predictable behavior pattern emerges.

purpose of a plan of decentralization must be to liberate the positive energies of all concerned. Parents, teachers, supervisors, and district administrators all need more constructive authority." [10]

### Havelock's Three Major Strategic Orientations

Having surveyed the state of organizational change, Ronald G. Havelock concluded that (1) the administrator has a wide range of strategies available to him but that (2) nearly all of the strategies may be classified under three distinctive "strategic orientations." Thus, he was able to devise a classification scheme for strategies and tactics of organizational change in schools. [11]

### A. The problem-solving strategy orientation (P-S)

Organizational change can be viewed as the outcome of the process by which the organization goes about solving its problems. Havelock's version of the steps involved in problem solving are:

1. the organization senses a need.
2. it translates the need into a *problem* statement or *diagnosis*.
3. it then (a) *searches for ideas* and information; and (b) selects an *innovation* that is *adapted* to the diagnosed needs; and (c) *tries out* the innovation; and finally, (d) *evaluates* its effectiveness.

Since the focus is on the potential adopting organization and its needs, any outsiders who may be involved play a strictly consultative role. They can help find new ideas, for example, or they can help with the problem-solving process itself. However, the diagnosis is seen as a crucial step in the problem-solving process in which the *organization's participants* play a key role. Outside consultants who may be assisting should function in a nondirective (i.e., collaborative) manner, helping the organization to work out its own solution to a problem that has been diagnosed by the organization's members; they should not function as authoritative experts who solve the client's problem for him. Those who favor this orientation to innovation believe that changes initiated and applied by the organization's members will have stronger commitment from them, hence have better chances for more complete and enduring adoption.

[10] Mayor's Advisory Panel on Decentralization of the New York City Schools, *Reconnection for Learning: A Community School System for New York City* (New York: The Panel, 1967), pp. 2–3.
[11] Ronald G. Havelock, "Innovations in Education: Strategies and Tactics" (Ann Arbor, Michigan: Center for Research on Utilization of Scientific Knowledge, Institute for Social Research, The University of Michigan, 1971).

SIX PROBLEM-SOLVING STRATEGIES.   Havelock identified six separate strategies under the problem-solving orientation:

1. System self-renewal.   The concept underlying this strategy is that organizational systems can develop increasing capability to be engaged in a continuous process of changing and adapting to environmental influences. Unlike classical organizational theory (whose emphasis on stability tends to produce resistance to change) *the concept of organizational self-renewal views the adaptive process as a fundamental characteristic of successful organizations* that exist in environments characterized by rapid change. The goal is to develop increasingly adequate problem-solving mechanisms in the organization. This requires the involvement of the participants in such activities as recognizng need, making a diagnosis, and searching for solutions.

Self-renewal requires a highly collaborative, "open" style of functioning within the organizational system, quite unlike the impersonal, hierarchical conditions of bureaucracies. In order to achieve this kind of operating style, the members of the organization undertake to develop the necessary group process and human relations skills with the aid of qualified consultants.

The concept of organization self-renewal, largely the outcome of work by organizational psychologists, was first comprehensively described by Rensis Likert in 1961 [12] in a book that, as Marrow has said, envisioned . . . "a universally applicable continuously adaptive organizational system." [13] In 1969 Gordon Lippitt elaborated on the concept with a well-developed approach to the process of renewal based on the notion that every organization has a life cycle (birth-youth-maturity) with different renewal needs at each stage of its existence.[14]

Matthew B. Miles has provided a brief but incisive description of the concept as it was applied in the Cooperative Project for Educational Development.[15] By the early 1970s among the most clearly elaborated and systematic approaches to applying the concept of self-renewal to organizations was Blake and Mouton's Managerial Grid,[16] though their work

[12] Rensis Likert, *New Patterns of Management* (New York: McGraw-Hill Book Company, 1961).
[13] Alfred J. Marrow, David G. Bowers, and Stanley E. Seashore, *Management by Participation: Creating a Climate for Personal and Organizational Development* (New York: Harper and Row, 1967), p. 231.
[14] Gordon L. Lippitt, *Organizational Renewal: Achieving Viability in a Changing World* (New York: Appleton-Century-Crofts, 1969).
[15] Matthew B. Miles and Dale G. Lake, "Self-Renewal in School Systems: a Strategy for Planned Change," in Goodwin Watson, ed., *Concepts for Social Change* (Washington, D.C.: National Training Laboratories, NEA, 1967).
[16] Robert R. Blake and Jane Srygley Mouton, *Building a Dynamic Corporation Through Grid Organization Development* (Reading, Mass.: Addison-Wesley Publishing Company, 1969).

was largely focused on business and industrial organizations. The Managerial Grid is discussed further in this book.

We feel that the other five strategies which Havelock identifies with the problem-solving orientation are actually a part of organization renewal. Though each of the strategies can stand by itself and be the central thrust of an organizational change effort, each is normally employed as a tactic by those attempting to implement the self-renewal approach. The other five strategies are:

2. Action research. Havelock describes action research as a collaboration of university social scientists with school personnel in diagnosing and solving problems; he makes it sound as though the school is used as a field site for the research of a professor from which both he and the school people might benefit.

3. Collaborative action inquiry. In Havelock's view, this features a more collegial relationship between professor and practitioner, both of whose efforts are deliberately focused on benefiting the cooperating school or system. It includes such activities as mutual goal-setting and sharing in the inquiry enterprise at all steps. Herbert Thelen, however, who according to Havelock elaborated the strategy, describes the process in terms strongly reminiscent of Kurt Lewin's original descriptions of action research (wherein the practitioner and the scientist collaborate on problem-solving, the use of force-field analysis to conceptualize the change problem, and a repeated cycle of diagnosis-action-assessment as a way to increase involvement over time).[17]

4. Human relations laboratory. This is the same as Katz and Kahn's Sensitivity Training strategy (see above).

5. Consultation. Havelock admits that *consultation* means so many things to so many people that it may not be appropriate to think of it as a strategy. However, he regards it as the activity of many behavioral science professors wherein they offer their services to organizations in a nonevaluative, nondirective, "helping relationship" capacity. The behavioral science consultant frequently models his role after the mental health consultant (e.g., the psychotherapist) in that he assists the client in defining and working on his own problem and provides him with feedback thought to be helpful in the process. Unlike the therapist, however, the consultant to the organization does not focus on individuals: his client is the organization.

The behavioral science consultant to organizations is often confused

---

[17] Herbert A. Thelen, "Concepts for Collaborative Action-Inquiry," in Goodwin Watson, ed., *Concepts for Social Change* (Washington, D.C.: National Training Laboratories, NEA, 1967).

as to who is his client (e.g., is it the school system that is paying for his services or is it the superintendent of schools who hired him?). His role is made difficult when an administrator looks to the consultant for support in a conflict situation, while the consultant views the entire organization as his client.

6. Sharing of practice innovations.  This was the last strategy identified by Havelock under the problem-solving orientation to innovation in education. It involves sharing user-originated practices in the target organization. An example is the work of Ronald Lippitt in developing ways to facilitate the sharing of new teaching practices being developed by classroom teachers.

TACTICS OF THE PROBLEM-SOLVING ORIENTATION.  Havelock identified nine tactics that—while not limited to problem-solving strategies in their application—nonetheless are commonly employed in carrying such strategies out.

1. T-group (sensitivity training group).  As a tactic, the T-Group has numerous variants and approaches. Generally speaking, however, T-Groups are relatively unstructured groups that provide participants an opportunity to explore existing group functioning and to experiment with possible new roles for themselves in groups. Trust and openness are usually important values in such groups. The T-Group is an important component of so-called laboratory training.

2. Reflection.  Havelock applies this term to the nondirective approach of the consultant to client (or therapist to patient) in which the emphasis is on the client (e.g., organization) being actively involved in the processes of diagnosis of a problem and in seeking ways of solving it. According to Carl Rogers,[18] the intent is to develop a relationship to the client that facilitates learning, autonomy, and self-direction (as opposed to a relationship—such as doctor to patient or lawyer to client—in which the client becomes increasingly dependent upon the consultant for knowledge and direction). To achieve this, an important function of the consultant is to reflect back to the client the client's own thoughts and actions in ways that will facilitate the client's self-examination of what he is doing.

3. Authentic feedback.  This tactic differs from *reflection* in that it provides information to the client organization about the effect that its actions have upon other people or systems; reflection lets the client look

18 Carl R. Rogers, "The Characteristics of a Helping Relationship," *Personnel and Guidance Journal*, 37 (September 1958), 11–16.

at his own thoughts or actions while feedback gives him better information about the impact of things he is doing.

4. Role playing.   This practice is widely used in facilitating self-learning; there are numerous specialized techniques for using it in specific situations to ease problem-solving. Generally its function is to provide the client with reflective and feedback data.

5. Group observation and process analysis.   This widely used tactic helps a group analyze and discuss its own operating problems. Trained observers provide the group with analyses of what is happening in the group and thus open up for discussion and criticism behaviors within the group that would ordinarily be taboo.

6. The derivation conference.   This is one of many variants for systematically facilitating self-examination of the interpersonal functioning of a group. This particular approach, the derivation conference, is typical of such approaches in that it utilizes a series of problem-solving tactics with a temporary group comprised of representatives of various levels from the organization plus outside consultants who organize the conference and facilitate its operation. Again, such conferences typically utilize many problem-solving tactics combined into an overall design for learning.

7. Survey feedback.   This tactic, like Katz and Kahn's "data feedback," is based upon the methodologies developed by Floyd Mann.[19]

8. Brain storming.   This is a technique that encourages members of the group to generate many possible solutions to its problems while temporarily suspending concern for practicability of any of the proffered ideas. Brain storming is useful in dealing with problems of organizational change not only because it releases creative ideas in the group but also because it helps to develop the habit of searching for fresh ways of solving problems rather than relying merely on modifying or adapting existing practices.

9. Synectics.   This is the term coined by William Gordon [20] to designate his attempts to fuse brain storming with more traditional problem-solving techniques (such as experimentation) into a comprehensive process of organizational innovation. More a concept than a process at this stage

[19] Floyd C. Mann and Franklin W. Neff, *Managing Major Change in Organizations* (Ann Arbor, Mich.: The Foundation for Research on Human Behavior, 1961).
[20] William J. J. Gordon, *Synectics: the Development of Creative Capacity* (New York: Harper and Row, 1961).

of its development, it has had little actual application to practical situations.

## B. *The social interaction orientation (S-I).*

This strategic orientation is primarily concerned with the processes by which innovations spread through a social system from their original invention or discovery to their actual use by the consumer. Sociological research in the area of agricultural innovation has been very influential in popularizing this strategy.[21] As Havelock points out, "Usually the 'innovation' is a concrete item such as a fertilizer, a new kind of seed, a new drug, or a new curriculum package" [22] in the S-I change strategy. This helps to explain the popularity of conceptualizing "innovation" in the sense that Miles described, not only in agriculture but also in other fields, such as education.

The S-I approach is less than an intervention to bring about change than it is a conceptual framework by which the "natural" processes of the diffusion of innovations can be studied and understood. This understanding can provide guidance to those who wish to hasten the process of diffusing an innovation from its beginnings to widespread use. For example, the adopter of an innovation is not considered an isolated individual, but a person who is part of a complex network of social interrelationships; this social structure has powerful influence over the individual's behavior in dealing with innovations.

The individual who is involved at the center of a social network tends to adopt an innovation earlier than one who is on the periphery of things: he gets information early and he feels less need to wait and see what others will do. Late adopters, however, are usually relatively isolated from the communication network of the insiders: because they get information later, they want assurance that the new idea is going to be widely adopted by the leaders in the field before they go along with it.

Havelock believes that research in this area tends to support five generalizations about the process of diffusing innovations through a social system:

1. The individual belongs to a network of social relations (i.e., a social system) that has great influence on what he does about adopting an innovation.

[21] The reader will recognize that this is the strategic orientation favored by a number of people concerned with educational change, e.g., Brickell, Mort, Smith, and Orlosky (see above).
[22] Havelock, "Innovations in Education," p. 7.

2. One can predict whether an individual will tend to adopt an innovation early or lag in adopting it, based on his place in the network.

3. Informal contact between people in the social system is vital for influencing the behavior of an individual potential adopter.

4. The relationship of an individual to groups in the social system determines his adoption behavior.

5. There is a predictable curve that characteristically describes the diffusion of an innovation through a social system. The process starts out slowly, rapidly accelerates during a period of popularity, then slows down as it is finally completed.[23]

FOUR SOCIAL INTERACTION STRATEGIES. Because the S-I orientation to innovation has been such a popular one for the study of the "natural" processes whereby new ideas are disseminated and adopted, it might be argued that it has "generated relatively few explicit strategies or action alternatives." [24] There are, however, at least four approaches (that Havelock prefers to call "quasi-strategies") that clearly have strategic implications; all of them have been widely utilized in American education.

1. Natural diffusion. This approach suggests simply that there is a "natural" process by which innovative ideas are spread. This process is relatively predictable in the way it develops:

> After an invention which is destined to spread throughout the school appears, fifteen years typically elapse before it is found in 3 per cent of the school systems . . . After practices have reached the 3 per cent point of diffusion their rate of spread accelerates. An additional 20 years usually suffices for an almost complete diffusion in an area the size of an average state. There are indications that the rate of spread throughout the nation is not much slower.[25]

Accordingly, Paul Mort reasoned, the average school lags about twenty-five years behind the leaders in adopting new practices. There are indications that this process has speeded up since the 1950s but it is difficult to say to what extent. The pattern, however, still remains relatively predictable:

> After a very extended early period of testing, development, trial and error, and sporadic localized adoption, innovations diffuse in a remarkably regular pattern. Indeed, when 10 to 20% have adopted an innovation, the

23 Ibid.
24 Ibid., p. 8.
25 Paul R. Mort, "Educational Adaptability," in Donald H. Ross, ed., *Administration for Adaptability* (New York: Metropolitan School Study Council, 1958), pp. 32–33.

forces of social interaction are such that the vast majority of the rest of the society will soon follow.[26]

2. Utilizing communication networks to facilitate the diffusion process. Since the social interaction orientation depends upon the communication of ideas and their acceptance by others, it is important to seek ways to enhance this part of the diffusion process. Obviously, such things as knowing who the opinion-makers are and with whom they communicate in the social system is essential to facilitate the diffusion of an innovation. This leads to the complex task of understanding the formal and the informal networks in the social system and using the knowledge effectively to ease acceptance of the innovation. Sometimes this means such obvious things as keeping the superintendent of schools and the school principals well-informed. But the informal side of the organization's social system must not be overlooked, either: certain teachers, parents, para-professionals, and others often play influential roles in communicating new ideas to people in the social system, even though they have no official power or authority over others in the organization.

A near-strategy for organizational change, at least, lies in (a) studying and analyzing the effective communication networks in the organization, both formal and informal, and (b) making effective use of this awareness to establish and direct communication that is intended to bring change about. A very common and simple illustration of this may be found in the typical principal-faculty conferences that take place in most schools on a regular basis. One central reason for holding such meetings is to provide for communication, especially from the principal to the teachers. Yet there is considerable evidence to support the belief that, too often, very little communication is actually achieved in this setting. Studies have repeatedly shown that the teachers often feel literally excluded, not only by the topics being dealt with (that are frequently thought by teachers to be wrong ones) but also by the apparently widespread belief of principals that communication is basically a one-way proposition. Careful, productive listening is very much an active (not a passive) involvement, of course, and the principal who studies and understands the communication processes in his meetings with teachers is in a better position to utilize this official communication channel more effectively.

On the other hand, one must not ignore the informal communication channels that exist in every school as well as all other organizations. As long as the administrator concentrates on the official, formal channels

[26] Havelock, "Innovations in Education," p. 9. Perhaps the best discussion of this process, to which Havelock also refers, is Everett M. Rogers, *Diffusion of Innovations* (New York: The Free Press, 1962).

open to him—such as faculty conferences, memoranda, and supervisory post-observation conferences with teachers—and fails to utilize the informal communication networks, his communication is very limited. There are key people in the coffee klatches, the lunch groups, the cliques, the job-alike groups, and departments who—unofficially and informally —carry great weight with others, know many people, and are crucial to the spreading of ideas, attitudes, and beliefs in the organization. Understanding this and identifying the informal networks of these people is essential if the administrator hopes to utilize the full range of communication channels that are available to help spread knowledge of new ideas through the organization's social system.

At this point it is necessary to interject a warning: in our traditionally hierarchical school organizational environments, we tend to think of communication as a downward-oriented process in which good ideas are passed on to the lower ranks for action. The S-I orientation to change reinforces this somewhat, with its emphasis on the development of the innovation outside of the organization; the role of communication is to disseminate knowledge of the innovation. *This is a point that clearly differentiates the social-interaction approach from the problem-solving approach* described earlier.

However, emphasis on social system concepts (that underly all major research into the diffusion of innovations through social systems) stresses the importance of informal relationships as a means of communication within the organization. The concept is one of freely-functioning networks that facilitate the movement of ideas and knowledge from the lower ranks of the organization upward—and horizontally, too— as well as downward from higher administrative levels. The point is that these informal networks of people exist and are functioning in the social systems that we call organizations. The integration of formal networks with informal networks is, in the systems view, a crucial function of administration.

3. Network building.   This strategy goes beyond mere recognition that social systems have communications networks through which innovative knowledge is transmitted: it calls for the development of specially designed network structures to do the job faster and better. The example that has been studied and copied worldwide is that of the so-called "agricultural model," particularly the Cooperative Extension Service of the United States Department of Agriculture with its ubiquitous County Agent.

Using both formal and informal means, ranging from public meetings to radio talks, from trouble-shooting out in the fields to demonstration plots in convenient locations, from working with youth groups to participating in county fairs, the Extension Service deliberately attempts to facilitate communication about new and better practices among farmers. A key aspect in the effort has been to use local leaders—because they are trusted and respected by their neighbors more than "outsiders" who claimed to be "experts"—in such crucial activities as giving demonstrations and speaking at informational meetings.

Network building has been successful in other fields; the "detail men" employed by drug companies are often seen as playing a role comparable to the county agent in linking members of the medical profession to the technology of medicine. Paul Mort and his associates were building networks when they linked school systems together by forming such organizations as the Associated Public School Systems and the Metropolitan School Study Council, that led directly to the establishment of numerous other school study councils across the nation. Many of these councils have deliberately employed approaches utilized by the Agricultural Extension Service, especially the use of local leaders.

4. Multi-media approaches. The fourth quasi-strategy that Havelock categorizes under the social-interaction orientation includes the use of many media, especially mass media, to facilitate communication in advertising campaigns. Havelock seems to feel that different approaches and different media, properly synchronized to the various stages of the dissemination process (e.g., awareness, interest, trial, evaluation, and adoption)—in the manner of commercial marketing techniques—would be a useful strategy in education.

TACTICS OF THE SOCIAL INTERACTION ORIENTATION. Havelock has identified five tactics that he feels are commonly associated with S-I strategies. All of these tactics are, of course, focused on the problem of facilitating communication and acceptance of innovative ideas through the complex network of people who comprise a social system.

1. *Mass media dissemination* is useful for rapidly reaching those individuals in the social system who are leaders in opinion formation. This tactic is most effective fairly early in the dissemination process when it is important to make people aware of an innovation. Thus, for example, when the United States Office of Education underwrote its first experimental use of the "voucher system" in La Jolla, California in 1972, the extensive coverage of the event that was sought in the print and electronic media could be partially interpreted as attempts to communicate knowledge of the innovation to other potential early adopters across the country.

2. *The "County Agent,"* so clearly identified with the United States

Agricultural Extension Service, has become a model for "change agents" around the world in many kinds of situations. Basically, it is the concept that a particular individual in residence has the task to link the local people to the sources of innovative ideas in very practical, workable ways. While the county agent operates in numerous formal ways—such as organizing meetings, issuing publications, and arranging demonstrations—an important part of his impact comes about by being involved in the local social system in numerous informal ways. Thus, the county agent becomes highly influential by getting to know many people (especially opinion leaders) and communicating knowledge and ideas to them informally—perhaps in a casual conversation out in a farmer's field or at a chance encounter at a local cooperative meeting. He extends his influence by using such activities as meetings and demonstrations to maximize the impact that opinion leaders have upon others in the social system.

3. *The salesman* can, under certain conditions, fulfill a role remarkably similar to that of the county agent. Every school administrator knows what the effect will be when a salesman with a new product shows him that certain prestigious schools and educators are already using the product with success. Although they may be motivated basically by the hope of personal profit, salesmen can serve a useful function in increasing communication about innovations among busy educators.

4. *Prestige suggestion* as a S-I tactic involves telling an individual that some respected colleague or group is using an innovation. The implication is clear: if the opinion leader approves the innovation, then it is worth serious consideration by later adopters. The tactic is, of course, used in the world of advertising and leads to often strenuous efforts to "line up" well-known educators, schools, and school districts in favor of an innovative idea (e.g., by their purchasing the books or equipment) in the belief that the rest of the field will fall in line. The United States Office of Education and the Office of Economic Opportunity have pursued this tactic vigorously in attempts to sell new ideas to school districts quickly.

5. *Opinion leadership utilization* involves influencing key leaders in certain fields to support certain innovations with the hope that the natural workings of the S-I system will result in wide adoption. Although such a tactic may have been effective in some fields, it has not been so in American public education. One probable reason is that there are few leaders in public education with the stature necessary to influence a very wide following. In the post-World War II years up into the 1970s, at least, American public education has been more notable for its diversity of leadership and factionalized debate than it has for

the presence of clear influence by widely respected leadership. In this volatile situation it has been difficult to identify any set of leaders whose opinions could do more than set off fresh discussion and debate.

## C. Research, Development, and Diffusion Orientation (R, D, & D)

This is the last of the three strategies for innovation in education identified by Havelock. The orientation of this strategy, as Havelock states it, is based upon five assumptions:

1. That there is a rational, orderly, sequence of events that marks the development of an innovation, its adoption, and widespread application in practice. The sequence of events normally includes (a) research (invention or discovery of the idea), (b) development of the idea into practical, useful products, (c) packaging of the products (e.g., into kits, books, films or tapes), and (d) mass dissemination.

2. Large-scale planning for a significant time-frame is required to bring about the unfolding of the R, D, & D sequence in an orderly, effective way.

3. There must be an appropriate division of labor to carry out each phase of the sequence and the efforts of the various specialized divisions must be coordinated according to the plan. The general idea here is to utilize the particular skills and talents of specialized people to the maximum. Thus, researchers are not expected to develop and package their ideas, nor are practitioners expected to conduct research.

4. The potential adopter will play a rational but relatively passive role in the process, accepting and adopting the innovation if it is offered to him under the proper conditions.

5. There are likely to be very high initial costs in this process, in the research and development phases particularly. However, the anticipated high quality of the product coupled with its utilization on a mass basis will eventually bring the unit-cost down, resulting in a high level of economic efficiency.

This strategy for innovation is, of course, widely used in industry, agriculture, military organizations, and other groups. Thus we see computer manufacturers plowing enormous sums of money into research, development, and dissemination efforts necessary to bring forth new and better products in the belief that customers will buy them and thus offset the initial costs, return a profit to the manufacturer and, at the same time, better meet the customer's needs. As we have pointed out, it is a strategy that has been employed notably in American agriculture fully justifying—in the eyes of many people—the enormous costs of maintaining the research, development, and dissemination enterprises represented by such institutions as the land-grant colleges, agricultural experiment stations, and the agricultural extension services. Examples of R, D, & D strategy readily come to mind in the fields of medicine in which the findings of researchers are interpreted in terms of specific applications and procedures; after testing and refinement, the products necessary for the applications and procedures are mass produced and disseminated for use on patients by practitioners.

R, D, & D STRATEGY. The R, D, & D orientation is, essentially, a strategy in itself. While Havelock suggests the possible identification of a few variants on the strategy, the usual approach is to develop high-performance products that are intended to implement the research-based innovation or discovery in a relatively complete and technically correct fashion. This suggests the creation of a technological system of inter-related products, complete with detailed instructions for applying and utilizing them under various anticipated possible conditions. Thus, it is not enough to develop a new type of fertilizer and find ways to persuade people to use it. The new product must be packaged so that a farmer can buy it readily and use it confidently, with specific directions and the necessary tools included as part of the package (or otherwise readily available) so that the product will be used correctly and will yield the desired results. So it is with a new medicine, with which the physician is only vaguely familiar or a new kind of paint that the craftsman never used before. The performance of the product is, in no small part, ascribable to the attempt to make the product "user-proof" in the hands of even those who may be relatively inept or careless.

In education, such high-performance products often take the form of "packaged" curriculums, such as the BSCS and SMSG programs or some of the foreign language programs that are designed to be applied as-is by the teacher without alteration, rearrangement, or deletion. Less ambitious high-performance teaching products often take the form of "instructional units", typically including coordinated hard-copy materials, visuals, audio and video tapes, manipulable objects, together with the omnipresent teachers' guides that help the teacher coordinate the program according to an overall design. As school administrators are well aware, coordinating the overall application of high-performance educational products into a well-orchestrated school-wide effort is no small task in the presence of the wide range of personal variables and the dynamic interpersonal milieu usually found in most schools. Performance contracting emerged in the late 1960s as one possible response to this problem: many such efforts were attempts to utilize high-performance instructional products on a comprehensive scale previously unmatched in most public school organizations.

TACTICS OF THE RESEARCH, DEVELOPMENT, AND DIFFUSION ORIENTATION. A set of tactics fundamental to this orientation to innovation is related to research. Thus, there is interest in constantly promoting better and more adequate research into the problems that plague the schools and public education.

Improving the analysis, design, and execution of educational research efforts is fundamental to purposeful change in schools Therefore, activities intended to improve the quality and breadth of educational research are basic R, D, & D tactics: ranging from the study of improved statistical techniques to the reexamination of hoary assumptions that have been the springboard for action in education for generations. Such fundamental research as Guilford's work on the nature of intellect, Piaget's investigations into the cognitive development of children, Jensen's controversial study of a possible relationship between ethnicity and measured intellectual ability, and Coleman's classic analysis of the effects of schooling in equalizing educational opportunity followed by Jencks's re-analysis of the same problem may well be regarded—in the R, D, & D view of educational change—as representative of the research that is crucial to meaningful planned change in American schools. This is precisely the point of view that motivated many people to support the establishment of the National Institute of Education in the tradition of the National Institutes of Health: to stimulate more and better quality basic research into fundamental educational problems so that development of educational products and practices could be redesigned basically rather than merely tinkered with on an ad hoc basis.

However, practicing school teachers and administrators have only a general and superficial knowledge of such research—just as medical practitioners have a relatively superficial knowledge about the most advanced current research techniques in their fields. To have practical effect in bringing about change in the operation of public schools, it is necessary that two tactics be brought into play:

1. *Development* of the knowledge and innovative approaches into some packageable, portable form.
2. *Diffusion* of the package—the innovation—to a wide audience of potential adopters in a way that will enhance the likelihood that they will, in fact, adopt the new approach.

Following are illustrations of such tactics.

1. Experimental demonstration.   One of the tried-and-true techniques for facilitating the diffusion of an innovation, this approach has the advantage of letting the adopter see for himself. The more ideal the con-

ditions under which the demonstration is conducted, the less effective it is likely to be. Practitioners appear to be more readily convinced when they see an innovation being tried under conditions much like their own. Special projects with high budgets, selected personnel, and other "model" conditions do not usually have great impact. A project in a nearby school district, however, facing conditions well known to the potential adopter is more likely to have greater effect.

2. Translation. In this case the research findings are expressed in practical language, simplified, and generalized so that they can be discussed more readily in terms of programs and action. We often hear basically inaccurate statements about using the *findings* of research in efforts to improve the schools. Practitioners find the *concepts* emerging from research useful, and it is these that they seek to learn and implement in practical ways. Translation, as a tactic for disseminating innovation, *is most useful when it deals with concepts emerging from research*—basically generalizations—rather than when it attempts to deal with the findings of specific research, which are always limited and circumscribed by the specific conditions of the particular investigations under consideration. A goal of translation, then, is to develop useful concepts from the findings of a number of research studies, that comprise a substantial body of scientific literature.

3. Packaging. Havelock feels that this is a phase of the diffusion process that has been badly neglected in educational R, D, & D, still being in a primitive stage as compared with the commercial world. Packaging includes imaginative, colorful, complete integrated presentations that involve various media in a way that is powerful, simple to use, and rich in variety.

Ultimately, success of the R, D, & D orientation to educational innovation must rest upon (a) a well-developed and systematic division of labor in which specialists perform the particular tasks for which they are best equipped, (b) the existence of a comprehensive diffusion system that enables rapid communication with minimum distortion, and (c) a highly adequate dynamic system of coordinated communication linking all levels of the specialists within the system. This linkage is seen by Havelock as crucial to the process, and is marked by a highly collaborative approach, mutual trust and respect among the various specialized contributors to the process, and adequate feedback processes—not only between individuals in the system but also between different groups. In short, to be effective, the R, D, & D enterprise must be a *system* in every sense of the word: specialized elements, well coordinated, with clear goals, with the interdependent units aware of what the total enterprise consists and what their function in it is.

### Chin and Benne's General Strategies for Effecting Change

One of the most popular attempts to identify and classify strategies of organizational change is that of Robert Chin and Kenneth D. Benne.[27] They developed a three-part typology into which they grouped various approaches to change according to the fundamental assumptions upon which they are based. They labeled the three types as follows: (1) empirical-rational strategies, (2) normative-reeducative strategies, and (3) power-coercive strategies.

*Empirical-rational strategies*

These are predicated upon two basic assumptions: first, that people (individually or in groups) are rational and, second, that they pursue their own self-interest (as they perceive it). Therefore when knowledge of some new and better way of doing things that is harmonious with the self-interest of the individual or the group is discovered, it will probably be adopted. The logic and rationality of this approach has been so fundamentally appealing in modern times to people in the western world that it has been a highly popular approach to change. Thus, research, study, and methodical universal education have greatly increased the likelihood that knowledge and reason would be used as springboards to action in the conduct of one's affairs. Public education in the United States—from the establishment of the common school philosophy, to the efforts by John Dewey to emphasize the utility of the scientific method in the solution of man's problems, to the intellectual elitism of the post-Sputnik era—has consistently woven variations on this theme. Much of management science—as pioneered by such leaders as Frederick Taylor, Henri Fayol and even Woodrow Wilson—springs from this empirical-rational view.

Chin and Benne identify five change strategies under the empirical-rational rubric:

1. BASIC RESEARCH AND DISSEMINATION OF KNOWLEDGE THROUGH GENERAL EDUCATION.    According to Chin and Benne, this strategy (essentially R, D, & D), seems especially appropriate for "thing technologies" that are perceived to be generally acceptable by the target population of potential adopters. This point is illustrated by the widespread support for research in the control of certain diseases—such as polio, cancer, and heart disease.

---

[27] Robert Chin and Kenneth D. Benne, "General Strategies for Effecting Changes in Human Systems," in Warren G. Bennis, Kenneth D. Benne, and Robert Chin, eds., *The Planning of Change*, 2nd ed. (New York: Holt, Rinehart and Winston, Inc., 1969).

Once the research has developed the necessary knowledge, then the development phase focuses on "packaging" the innovation for practical use, and finally education programs of various kinds induce people to adopt the innovation (e.g., have their children immunized, stop smoking, and reduce cholesterol content of the diet.) But those innovations that are not generally popular are not so easily accepted. Chin and Benne illustrate this with the case of fluoridation of public water supplies to help solve the problem of dental caries. Because there has not been broad readiness for the innovation, the diffusion phase of the strategy has met with spotty success. Rogers describes the failure of an effort to persuade the peasants of a South American country to boil their unsafe drinking water, despite the best efforts of trained change agents and a relatively well-developed program.[28] The people in the target social system must have a certain readiness to adopt new knowledge—indeed, see a genuine need for it—before it will be accepted and acted upon.

2. PERSONNEL SELECTION AND REPLACEMENT. This strategy can be incremental, in the sense that new standards or new criteria may be established in filling normal personnel needs due to attrition or growth of the organization. Reformers often try to decrease personnel through such means as offering early retirement, dismissal, abolishing positions, transfers, and various reorganizaiton schemes. Chin and Benne feel that this strategy has not been especially beneficial partly because emphasis on individual role occupants as the cause of difficulty often masks the social or systemic problems that are actually at issue.

3. SYSTEMS ANALYSIS. As Chin and Benne view it, this strategy has actually been applied in organizations in the tradition of Taylor's early scientific management with emphasis on conventional bureaucratic concepts of efficiency. The recent trend toward inclusion of behavioral scientists in systems analysis work— along with engineers and mathematicians —may have promise for broadening the utility and effectiveness of this strategy, taking more adequately into account the human (e.g., social and psychological) aspects of organization in addition to the traditional technical-structural-operational aspects.

4. APPLIED RESEARCH AND LINKAGE SYSTEMS FOR DIFFUSION OF RESEARCH RESULTS. This is the strategy of deliberately establishing a linkage system for the development and diffusion of new knowledge developed through research. Not surprisingly, Chin and Benne use the American agricul-

[28] Everett M. Rogers, *Diffusion of Innovations* (New York: The Free Press, 1962), Chapter I.

tural model as an illustration—featuring such elements as the network comprised of the land-grant university, the cooperative extension service, and the county agent as readily visible parts of the linkage system.

5. UTOPIAN THINKING AS A CHANGE STRATEGY. Rational, empirical attempts to project our thinking ahead to what *might* exist in the future, what the alternatives may be, and what *ought* to be at that future time can lead to planned efforts to direct the course of events toward some desired goal, rather than to accept whatever may occur. This concept was popularized for many Americans by Alvin Toffler in the 1960s through his best-selling book, *Future Shock*.

The field of *futurism,* though relatively new, has attracted a diverse group of scholars and planners representing various disciplines and is building a substantial body of literature in such potentially useful areas as developing scientific techniques for improving forecasting of the future. So-called think tanks often involve themselves in this sort of activity. The notion is, of course, based upon the highly rational premise that our skill at predicting the future can be helpful in making decisions at the present time—which is quite a different thing from using emotionally tinged normative statements of a utopian nature as a guide to change.

### Normative-reeducative strategies of change

These are based on quite a different perception of man in his environment than the empirical-rational strategies. The empirical-rational orientation stresses (a) the role of rationality of man with its emphasis on logic and reason as determinants of behavior, and (b) the individual as a decision maker in pursuing his own self-interests. By contrast, the normative-reeducative view takes into account man's need to satisfy his nonrational feelings and to interact dynamically with his environment (both human and physical) as he relates to it.

The roots of the normative-reeducative orientation lie principally in the development of psychology as a discipline. In this century, psychology has developed in three principal mainstreams or schools of thought: (a) Freudian psychology, (b) behaviorism, and (c) humanistic psychology; of course, both behaviorism and humanistic psychology (sometimes called the "third school" of psychology) partially spring from the earlier work of the Freudian school. The normative-reeducative approach to change flows naturally from certain views often associated with humanistic psychology, as described by such well-known scholars as Kurt Lewin, Abraham Maslow, Rollo May, and Carl Rogers. Important roots are traceable to two other significant sources: (1) the John Dewey philosophy of education, with its emphasis on active involvement of the individual in his own learning and the function of the group in the learning process; and (2) industrial sociology, as pioneered by Elton Mayo's work in the Western Electric studies, that underscored the role of the work-group in shaping organizational behavior.

These roots have been brought together and consolidated in the years since World War II in a number of interesting and powerful ways. One was the collaboration between Ronald Lippitt (a student of Kurt Lewin's) and Leland Bradford and Kenneth Benne (both students of John Dewey) that led to the establishment of the National Training Laboratories (and the first T-Group training at Bethel, Maine) in 1947. This beginning quickly attracted others from related fields and similar backgrounds, leading to considerable activity in group psychotherapy and the so-called "human potential" movement, as well as in the field of organizational change. In addition to Bethel, such names as Synanon (the drug rehabilitation center) and the Esalen Institute at Big Sur in California are among the better-known of the many (and very diverse) centers that are based directly on these roots.

Of course, some of these are primarily concerned with group counseling or psychotherapy; others are basically concerned with educating or training individuals for various purposes. Our interest in this work, however, is neither of these. We seek to learn what application the normative-reeducative strategy may have for changing schools.

In dealing with problems of organizational functioning, a central concept of the normative-reeducative orientation is that of the organization as a *human social system,* rather than as a technical system. This has led to a useful analogy between a consultant organizational specialist and the helping relationship that counselors seek to establish with individuals.

The counselor does not normally tell the individual what the problem is, nor does he give the individual the solution. His role is usually viewed as that of a skillful facilitator who can help the individual to recognize a problem and to work out ways of solving it, providing resource information when it is appropriate. The process is seen, essentially, as a learning process through which the individual grows in his own problem-solving abilities and, thus, increases in his ability to meet new challenges. The view is, of course, that one must actively participate in his own learning about himself so as to develop greater awareness and control of his own inner resources.

The counselor to the organization, or change agent, is usually known simply as a consultant; his intervention into the ongoing affairs of the client organization has many characteristics similar to those of an individual-to-counselor relationship: the relationship should be mutually collaborative in which roles and functions are clearly maintained, and the problems dealt with must be those of the client organization rather than someone else's. Central to the approach is the notion that—although the organization's problem may well be technical—it is possible that certain nonrational characteristics of the people within the organization (e.g., their attitudes and beliefs) may be very much involved in the problem; these must be exposed and dealt with. That is, if the normative values of the people in the social system have a causative relationship to organizational problems, then reeducation must be in the normative realm, not the technical realm. Thus, the label *normative-reeducative*.

From the establishment of the National Training Laboratories in 1947 until the late 1960s the focus of those engaged in normative-reeducative techniques, such as sensitivity training, was primarily on the individual—helping him become aware of his own feelings and attitudes, learning how they affect him and his dealings with others, helping him to develop and practice new and potentially more effective behavior patterns, and so on. Little direct thought was given to working with organizations, as such; it was believed that by helping people to learn to function in more effective ways, an organization would be helped indirectly to function better. By 1960 the recognition was spreading that where *organizational* functioning was the primary concern it would be more effective to apply normative-reeducative processes to the organization's social system itself. In recent years, there has been a rapid development of intervention techniques and processes suitable for change agents to use with a client organization as a system in a normative-reeducative way.

Thus, two basically different approaches that utilize the normative-reeducative orientation can be used as strategies of organizational change. They are complementary and in some ways parallel to each other.

1. IMPROVING THE PROBLEM-SOLVING CAPABILITIES OF THE SYSTEM. The point of view is that various symptoms (such as low productivity or poor morale) indicate that the organizational system is not solving its problems adequately, and that if it can be helped to function better in this regard, it will achieve its goals more adequately. While some change agents still tend to view such problems as almost exclusively dealing with the social system, it is generally recognized that one cannot separate this aspect of the organization from the technical problems that the organization must consider. Thus, the organization is not *either* a social system *or* a technical system but can be usefully viewed as a sociotechnical system; whatever efforts are made to improve the problem-solving capability of the organization must be carried out in the broader context that this implies.

2. FACILITATING THE PERSONAL GROWTH AND CREATIVITY OF THE INDIVIDUAL PERSONS WHO ARE IN THE SOCIAL SYSTEM. One of the telling criti-

cisms of organizations—especially bureaucracies—is that they are deadening to their human participants by demanding conformity and regimentation. There is evidence that an organization can be changed as a secondary outcome by a normative-reeducative approach to the basic unit in its human social system: the individual person. Under modern conditions of rapid social and technological change this approach enhances the organization's ability to respond satisfactorily to new problems by populating it with adaptive individuals who are able to cope adequately with the new ideas and demands.

This, of course, challenges and calls into question most of the conventional wisdom of administration and the notions of classical organizational theory with their strong emphasis on formal organization and top-to-bottom pyramidal control. Reeducative activities that seek to stimulate a collaborative rather than competitive relationship between people in the organization, that bring conflict into the open as something to be dealt with rather than avoided, that encourage people to find increasing satisfaction from their work—such activities inevitably suggest some sort of organizational system quite different from conventional bureaucracy. They suggest the need for a new pattern of administration that will help to keep people growing instead of keeping them in their place.

Reeducation of this kind cannot be accomplished under the conditions that have long prevailed in American in-service teacher education. In the first place, the conventional master-to-learner relationship—such as is standard fare in the courses, lectures, and workshops in the typical program of teacher education—tends to reinforce strongly the existing system, including the teacher's dependency role and low status in the organizational hierarchy. Group process training is coming into increasing use, however, to supplement the need for technical reeducation that conventional course work can meet. The thrust of the training—when used as an organizational change strategy—is to develop new normative standards of behavior in the organization's social system. These standards will emphasize openness in dealing with conflict, cooperation instead of competition, and an environment that encourages creativity and adaptation to change in contrast to the traditional bureaucratic concept of maintaining existing procedures and awaiting orders from the hierarchy. Such a process can change an organization's basic character from seeking to maintain a status quo to seeking to meet changing conditions in a dynamic fashion.

## Power-coercive approaches to change

The third general strategy for change identified by Chin and Benne rests upon certain assumptions regarding the use of power to influence human (hence, organizational) behavior. Knowledge is, for example, a source of power; it is used, of course, in the rational-empirical approach as a major element in bringing about change. Knowledge—particularly technical knowledge concerning such matters as group behavior and motivation—is an important source of power in the normative-reeducative approach, too. The power-coercive approach differs from either the rational-empirical or the normative-reeducative approaches in its willingness to use *sanctions* in order to obtain compliance from organizational participants.

Coercive power may range from actual threats to life, to physical compulsion, to sanctions of a political, moral, or professional nature. In schools the power-coercive approach to change as used here tends to emphasize the use, or the threat of use, of political and/or economic sanctions in order to produce the behaviors that the power-holder feels are appropriate.

For example, school administrators have found it rather easy to make beginning teachers "forget all that stuff they taught you at college" by making it plain that reappointment, desirable teaching schedules, and other rewards will depend on how well these teachers conform to local expectations. Similarly, federally funded projects that offer special financial assistance to school districts can exert powerful influence on local decisions.

It is entirely possible for people in the system to be influenced and controlled by such means and remain quite unaware of the extent to which they are responding to coercive power being exercised upon them. The exercise of coercive power is so much a part of our experience that we frequently are unaware of its influence in our lives.

The central point to emphasize in this strategy for change is its fundamental reliance upon the use of sanctions—actual or potential—to achieve its aims. Rationality, reason, human dynamics in the organizational system—all are secondary in the power-coercive point of view to the capability for effecting desired changes directly through the exercise of power.

USE OF POLITICAL POWER. One way of exercising legitimate political power is by gaining control of political institutions. The resultant passage of legislation, pronouncement of executive orders, and consonant court decisions can lend great weight to change efforts. There are many who believe that political power is the essential key to significant educational change in America. Its exercise, usually interpreted in terms of legislative or judicial orders accompanied by financial sanctions, is commonly viewed as having great influence to bring about change in schools.

However, a review of the history of the attempts to bring about major change in the public schools of the United States in the 1950s and 1960s raises serious questions as to the real impact of this strategy. Much as Supreme Court decisions, new laws, and administrative action by powerful political administrators—such as budget reshuffling—may please the reformers who worked hard to achieve the action, there remains the problem of actually changing the experience that students encounter in their classrooms. All too often, despite lavishly expensive new programs and drastic efforts to eliminate old practices, the educational experience of children is remarkably unaltered. In part this is because political and economic coercion (1) do not create new knowledge to make the desired goal achievable nor (2) do they solve the problem of providing the human beings in the schools with the new skills, attitudes, and value commitments that are essential to carrying out the necessary changes. By 1970, certainly, questions were being raised in the United States as to the efficacy of attempting to change schools through the power of political institutions.

The answer does not seek to undermine the efficacy of coercive political power such as court orders to reorganize school districts, laws intended to limit the authority of school administrators, or the careful manipulating of funding to favor some programs over others in order to bring about change in the schools. But our response to recent decades of experience with such efforts should underscore the crucial need for linking such actions with very effective normative-reeducative change efforts in the schools in order to implement the desired political goal.

Our response must also consider whether or not there is a knowledge problem in implementing the mandate that is being forced by political action. In many cases, although the political goal may be quite clear, those who pass the laws or make the coercive rulings fail to grasp the simple fact that the knowledge necessary to carry them out may not yet exist.

RESTRUCTURING POWER ELITES TO BRING ABOUT CHANGE. It is well recognized that our society has a power structure in which relatively limited elite groups have extraordinary power to make things happen or to keep them from happening; these power elites have considerable coercive power to affect change. Instead of accepting the existing power structure as fixed and inevitable it is possible to try to change the power structure. If this is done—with power either shifting to new hands or being spread among more people—it is possible to use the existing power in efforts to achieve new goals.

This is illustrated, of course, by efforts on the part of minority groups to gain representation in the key decision-making groups concerning their schools: school boards, administrative and teaching positions, and boards that control finances particularly. Decentralization of urban school districts, for example, was seen by some as a way of breaking up old power elites and reconstituting them in different ways so that the minority-group citizens of inner cities could gain new power to bring about change in the schools.

Teachers, on the other hand—long maintained in a powerless and dependent state—have responded to these and other changes in the traditional power structure with attempts to manipulate the power structure to their own advantage. Far from willing to stand by while schools are involved in struggles by contending power elites, teachers have entered the struggle through their professional organizations and unions. Thus, the demands by teachers that they have a greater voice in decision-making—especially in matters affecting class size, work assignments, and job security—add a new dimension to the rearrangement of power elites in American public education.

NONVIOLENT POWER STRATEGIES. The coercive power of political activity and the manipulation of power elites lies largely in the socio-economic realm: the power to control tax levy funds, the power to threaten the job security of individuals, and the power to reduce the power of others (for example, by defeating them in elections). These threaten the economic well-being of the opposing power elites and the status of the individuals within the elite. Another strategy for challenging the forces in the power structure is through the use of nonviolent methods, that derive their power largely from moral sanctions: emphasizing the cruelty of the oppressors, impressing those in power with their own guilt, and showing the unfairness of the system.

Nonviolent demonstrations and protests appear to be useful in defining and popularizing a problem. In the American context they have often been seized upon as issues to serve the cause of those who seek increased political power; hence, nonviolent techniques exert not only overt moral sanctions but also possess at least latent political power. When directed at individual schools or school systems, nonviolent strategies appear often to be effective in bringing change. This may be due, at least in part, to the normative-reeducative impact that these methods have on the people in the school organization. On a larger scale, however—in such matters as redistributing tax levy funds on the basis of a new concept of equity—it would appear that their effectiveness is more limited. Because power-coercive strategies are identified with the ability and determination to use sanctions to induce participants to change, they are dependent upon a hierarchy of power to achieve their goals.

## SYNTHESIS

We turn now to consider how these analyses may be useful in the administration of planned organizational change in schools. Essentially, they are useful chiefly because they help the manager of change to formulate a clear conceptualization of how the critical factors in the change process interrelate. Systematic purposive coordination and management require such insight.

For practical purposes, we utilize Havelock's taxonomy of change strategies and tactics because it appears to be the most comprehensive and systematic available. There are three major strategic orientations of this analysis: (1) Problem-Solving (P-S), (2) Social-Interaction (S-I), and (3) Research, Development, and Diffusion (R, D, & D). Havelock has added that there may well be at least a fourth strategic orientation; however, since he has not described such a fourth classification, the basic three are the most useful in dealing with practical problems. Clearly, the knowledgeable administrator can develop a systematic plan for effecting organizational change utilizing any of these strategies. The tactics associated with each strategy become, of course, the bases for action intended to implement the strategy.

As we have pointed out, there are four key organization subsystems: technology, structure, human, and task. The application of change tactics to the organization must have impact upon each of these subsystems. For the purposes of analyses and planning, therefore, the administrator can utilize a simple matrix as shown in Fig. 4-2. Such a schema helps to raise issues and questions as to how the change effort is to be handled in reference to each of the key organization subsystems and what impact is sought in each of them.

Finally, the coordination and management of organizational change require the involvement of the participants. Planning and implementation of a change strategy must take into consideration which participants are to be involved and in what ways. In Fig. 4-3 we have included a suggestive list of participants that would probably be modified for use in planning for a specific school; it should be noted that the participants identified in the framework are not listed in any particular intended order. Tactics indicated in Fig. 4-3, too, are merely illustrative and would be fully identified in actual use. The main point of the framework shown in Fig. 4-3 is to provide a conceptual basis for systematic, orderly planning, management, and evaluation of the complex elements of an organizational change effort.

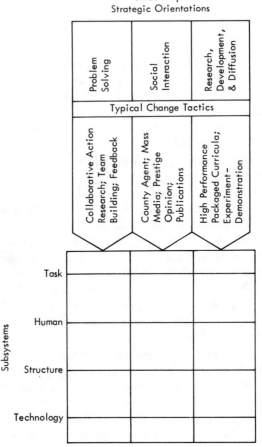

**Figure 4-2**
When change strategies are applied to an organization they interact with key
organizational subsystems.

## SUMMARY

There are four organizational subsystems that, using the systems concept
of organizational functioning, are fundamental to the administration of
change in schools: (1) task, (2) structure, (3) technology, and (4) people.
These subsystems provide the bases for developing a repertoire of administrative strategies and tactics for directing and controlling planned
organizational change.

The four organizational subsystems are interrelated in a highly

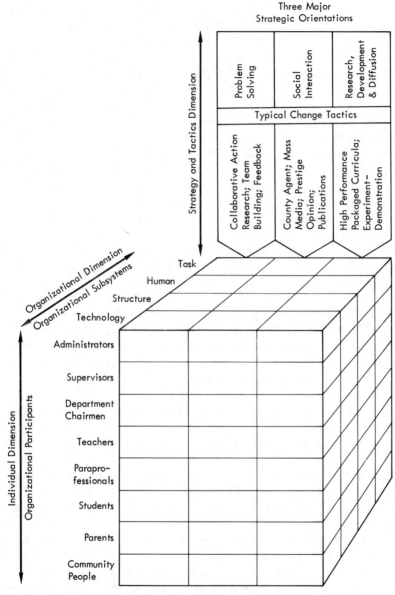

**Figure 4-3**
A framework for coordinating and managing organizational change in schools.

dynamic way: attempts to make significant changes in one will, perforce, produce complementary changes in the others. These may be either compensatory (i.e., adaptive) in nature or retaliative (i.e., alienative).

In the case of schools, goals are derived from the political realm. This has resulted in the schools having a number of diverse and sometimes conflicting goals and *tasks*. Organizational *structure* exists in the pattern of repeated human interactions in the organization, rather than in walls or membranes. Thus, the authority and power relationships between people in the organization, the patterns of communication among participants, and the nature of their role in decision-making delineate the organizational structure more clearly than a formalized "official" depiction of structure such as an organization chart. *Technology* refers to the tools required by the organization to perform its tasks. In addition to "hardware," this also includes inventions by which work processes are sequenced, scheduled and regulated. *People* refers to the human input into the organizational system, recognizing that the social culture of the system has powerful impact in shaping human behavior on the job. The affective aspects of the human input (e.g., fears, satisfactions, alienation, interest) are crucial in establishing the nature and quality of the social culture of a given organization.

Traditionally, attempts to bring about change in schools have been initiated primarily through alteration of the task; structural or technological variables with behavioral (i.e., "people") changes are seen as flowing from these primary efforts in a compensatory fashion. Thus, new goals are set, the school is reorganized, or new instructional processes are introduced with the expectation that teachers will adapt to the changes and learn to implement them. More recent developments, rapidly growing in popularity, stress bringing about change by first opening up opportunities for the organization's participants to share more effectively and responsibly in the functioning of the organization with the expectation that effective structural and technological changes will result from the more effective organizational behavior. The target of change is the organizational system, rather than individuals within the system. The dynamic interrelatedness of the school's subsystems and its exchange with its external environment emerge as centrally important in any approach to effecting change.

Although rational, logical, single cause-and-effect approaches to change have great popular appeal, their effectiveness is limited because they largely ignore the nonrational human elements of the organization. Behavioral science approaches, on the other hand, confront these factors as central concerns in administering change, by advocating tactics specifically designed to fully utilize the organization's human resources in identifying and solving problems. This view, in short, draws heavily on two main bodies of theory and knowledge:

1. Organizational analysis based upon general system theory.
2. Organizational behavior, especially as it deals with the conditions that help or hinder the motivation and skills that individuals in the school bring to coordinated group effort.

The goal is a self-renewing organization that

> . . . makes continuous, adaptive changes by maintaining a lively variety pool of resources and delicately monitoring its success in coping with the environment. It maintains openness to its environment, responsiveness among its internal subsystems and an open flow of its members' competencies in order to use its own resources as a district to cope with environmental change. In self-renewing organizations there is open, direct and clear communication. Conflict is seen as inevitable and natural and is brought out in the open so it can be used to bring about change instead of impeding work to be accomplished . . . Decisions are made by those who have the information instead of looking to those who have authority and emphasis is placed on the best possible decision. A self-renewing organization also has sensing processes and feedback mechanisms to tell which changes are needed.[29]

The concept of the self-renewing organization is probably the most powerful organizational change concept yet to emerge from the behavioral sciences. Because it is not widely known and accepted by educational administrators, this concept is the focus of our suggestions for further reading. In a sense, the concept of self-renewal is an umbrella under which other major behavioral concepts of organizational change may be subsumed.

The self-renewal approach to organizational change is emerging under the rubric of Organization Development that is described in the following chapter.

## SUGGESTED READING

Note: Leavitt, Likert and Lippitt are industry-oriented scholars. Their value to the interested reader lies in providing a systematic background to the behavioral science concepts underlying contemporary manage-

---

[29] *CASEA Progress Report* (Eugene, Oregon: Center for the Advanced Study of Educational Administration, University of Oregon, September 1972), p. 5.

ment. The last two suggested works attempt to analyze schools specifically in terms of behavioral concepts.

LEAVITT, HAROLD J. *Managerial Psychology.* 2nd ed. Chicago: The University of Chicago Press, 1964. Many more recent analyses of organizational behavior and the nonrational bases for management have been influenced by this work.

LIKERT, RENSIS. *New Patterns of Management.* New York: McGraw-Hill Book Company, 1961. A classic statement of the self-renewal concept. Though primarily concerned with profit-making firms, it elucidates fundamental concepts that the author feels are applicable to many kinds of organizations.

LIPPITT, GORDON L. *Organizational Renewal: Achieving Viability in a Changing World.* New York: Appleton-Century-Crofts, 1969. The author demonstrates that the renewal needs and processes for specific organizations vary over time as the organization evolves.

SARASON, SEYMOUR B. *The Culture of the School and the Problem of Change.* Boston: Allyn and Bacon, Inc., 1971. This scholarly small volume captures the essence of significant behavioral approaches to organizational analysis in an easy-to-read nontechnical style. Of special interest to educational administrators because it deals with realities of public schools in a straightforward manner.

WATSON, GOODWIN, "Toward a Conceptual Architecture of a Self-Renewing School System," in *Change in School Systems,* ed. by Goodwin Watson, pp. 106–115. Washington, D.C.: Cooperative Project for Educational Development, National Training Laboratories, N.E.A., 1967. Suggests a ten-part design for achieving self-renewal in school systems.

CHAPTER 5

# organization development
# and
# leader behavior

Organization Development (OD) is rapidly emerging as a major strategy
for helping organizations deal with demands for increased effectiveness
under contemporary conditions of change. It is, to a large extent, a
synthesis of the relevant behavioral science knowledge that has emerged
from the last half-century of research and experience.

"Organization development is a new approach, process and technology for effecting organization change and improvement and is based
on behavioral science principles and practices." [1] Being in the realm of
*applied* behavioral science, OD is very much concerned with the practical
application and utility of its tactics and processes to significant problems
of actual organizations. It has been utilized in a large number of widely
varying organizations, ranging from Esso Standard Oil to an American
Indian tribe, from the Foreign Service of the United States Department
of State to school systems, from Union Carbide, Boise Cascade, and
Polaroid Corporation to the National Aeronautics and Space Administration. Rapidly becoming popular in the United States, it is far from
being an American phenomenon: OD is widely established in highly
developed nations of Europe, Asia, and the Pacific, as well as in North
America.

The evolution of the central concepts underlying OD can be traced
to the 1940s. Kurt Lewin clearly laid the groundwork for OD in that

[1] Wendell French and Cecil Bell, "Comment," *Journal of Contemporary Business,* I (Summer 1972): 1.

decade through the development of some crucial concepts—such as the *field theory* of social psychology, the concept of *action research* in practical situations, and the *three-step cycle of organizational change*. As a field of practice, however, OD is of recent vintage: primitive attempts at what was to become OD are traceable only to the late 1950s. The first widely accepted books on the subject did not appear until 1969.[2] Since that time, however, the remarkable increase in the number of publications on OD—a few of the best being concerned with schools—attests to a significant upsurge in OD activity. Clearly, OD will rapidly increase in importance in administering change in schools in the near future, at least into the 1980s.

## THE NATURE OF ORGANIZATION DEVELOPMENT

Organization development has been defined in many ways. It is difficult to capture the full essence of such a comprehensive and complex approach to improving organizational effectiveness in a simple definition. Perhaps the most succinct yet comprehensive definition is that of French and Bell, who put it thus:

> organization development is a long-range effort to improve an organization's problem-solving and renewal processes, particularly through a more effective and collaborative management of organization culture . . . with special emphasis on the culture of formal work teams . . . with the assistance of a change agent, or catalyst, and the use of the theory and technology of applied behavioral science, including action research.[3]

As is so often the case with definitions of complex inventions, this lengthy statement—although inclusive—is most easily understandable to the reader who has some background in the field. Actually, OD rests upon a cluster of at least ten concepts that are very explicit. Taken together, these concepts form a comprehensive frame of reference or Gestalt that the administrator can use to understand better the processes of administering change through organization development.

### 1. The goal of OD

The focus of OD is primarily upon improving the functioning of the organization itself. Improving the productivity and effectiveness of the

[2] The widely used "six-pack" of paperbacks published as the *Addison-Wesley Series on Organization Development* (Reading, Mass.: Addison-Wesley Publishing Company, 1969).

[3] Wendell L. French and Cecil H. Bell, Jr., *Organization Development* (Englewood Cliffs, N.J.: Prentice-Hall, Inc., 1973), p. 15.

organization is seen as largely dependent upon developing the organization's capability to make better-quality decisions about its affairs—decisions affecting its structure, its use of technology, and its goals. The primary approach to this is to develop a work-oriented culture or climate in the organization that will maximize the involvement of the organization's people in more effective decision-making regarding matters of importance to them and to the goals of the organization.

Although OD may very well lead to the adoption of a new program or curriculum, or a restructuring of the organization, or commitment to new goals, these are not considered to be *first* steps to improved effectiveness of schools or school systems. Neither does OD assume—as some have speculated—that significant organizational change will result from programs limited to improving the personal and interpersonal skills of individuals or groups, whether through counselling, sensitivity training, conventional education or any other means. This is not likely to be enough to alter significantly established norms that shape the work-related behavior of the organization: rules, expectations, traditions, and habits.

## 2. System renewal

OD rejects the notion that entropy is inevitable in organizations. Stated positively, the view is that an organization can develop self-renewing characteristics, enabling it to increase its capability, adapt to change, and improve its record of goal achievement.

This concept of system self-renewal sees the organization not as being helplessly buffeted about by exigencies and changes thrust upon it, but as growing in its ability to initiate change, to have increasing impact upon its environment, and to develop increasing capability to adapt to new conditions and solve new problems over time. Perhaps more important is its ability to develop a growing sense of purpose and direction over time. The view is of an energized system marked by increasing vitality and imaginative creativity.

The self-renewal concept is at the center of the difference between organization *development* and organization *improvement*. The thrust is not merely to overcome some immediate problem and arrive at a new "frozen" state of organizational functioning. The concept is one of building into the organizational system the conditions, the skills, the processes, and the climate that foster *continual development* of the organization over a sustained period of time. Although OD may be triggered by a specific event—such as initiating a new school or facing up to community criticism—the event itself merely provides an entry point for action.

If OD techniques are used to develop responses to the event and then are dropped, rather than continued and extended, then the project is not OD at all but another piecemeal change effort so characteristic of public schools. The concept of management by crisis has become so firmly embedded in American educational administration that developing planned, systematic, sustained approaches is quite possibly the central problem of administering change in schools.

### 3. A systems approach

Organization development is based upon the concept of the organization as a complex sociotechnical system.[4] Such a view of the organization, of course, emphasizes the wholeness of the organizational system and the dynamic interrelatedness of its component subsystems: human, structural, technological, and task.

The school, for example, may be thought of as a system. It comprises subsystems, of course—departments, grade levels, informal groups, teams, and work groups—that are in a constant state of dynamic interrelationship. The school is also a subsystem of larger systems: the school district, for example, and the community in which it functions.

As we have described, such a view has fundamental implications for those concerned with administering organizational change; these are translated into certain fundamental assumptions:

a. To effect change that has long-range staying power one must change the system and not merely certain of its parts or subsystems.

b. Moreover, because of the dynamic interrelatedness and interdependency of the component subsystems, any significant change in a subsystem will produce compensatory or retaliatory changes in other subsystems.

c. Events very rarely occur in isolation or from single causes. Systems concepts of the organization emphasize the importance of dealing with events as manifestations of interrelated forces, issues, problems, causes, phenomena, and needs. The world of the organization is recognized as the complex system that it is, and ascribing single causation to phenomena or treating events as isolated incidents can mask our full understanding of them.

d. The organizational system is defined not by walls or membranes but by existing patterns of human functions. These patterns are not static, but are in constant dynamic equilibrium—as Lewin's concept of force field analysis illustrates. Therefore, the crucial information the administrator requires comes from analyzing the specific field of forces at

[4] The concept of sociotechnical system—that is, a view of the organization as integrating human systems and technical systems—has been developed by E. L. Trist of the Tavistock Institute. See, for example, E. L. Trist, "On Socio-Technical Systems," in Warren G. Bennis, Kenneth D. Benne, and Robert Chin, *The Planning of Change,* 2nd ed. (New York: Holt, Rinehart & Winston, 1969), pp. 268–82.

a particular time, rather than analyzing generalized historical data from the past or from other organizations.

## 4. Focus on people

The main concern for OD is the human social system of the organization, rather than task, technology, or structure dimensions. Specifically, the focus is upon the organizational culture that characterizes the climate of beliefs influencing behavior—such as the ways in which superordinates and subordinates deal with one another, the ways in which work groups relate to each other, and the extent to which people in the organization are involved in identifying organizational problems and seeking solutions to them. Attitudes, values, feelings, openness of communication, are typical concerns to OD. It matters what people think, how open their communication is, how they deal with conflict and to what extent they feel involved in their jobs, because these kinds of human concerns help determine how much work gets done and how well. People who have learned to keep their thoughts to themselves, to be discreet in proffering a new idea or in voicing doubt or criticism contribute little to the organization's ability to diagnose its problems and find solutions. The climate of many schools encourages this kind of behavior—leaving decisions to the upper echelons and frowning upon lower participants who "cause trouble" by raising questions.

Commonly, the school's climate carefully structures organizational behavior so as to minimize open, free, vigorous participation in central decisions—witness the typical faculty meeting with its crowded agenda of minutiae or the superintendent's pro-forma appearances before the staff, that are filled with routine platitudes. Organizations with such characteristics tend to be relatively inflexible, slow to change, and defensive in a fast-changing environment.

In the OD view, one of the great resources available to an organization trying to improve its effectiveness is its own people. By encouraging people to become involved, concerned participants rather than making them feel powerless and manipulated by unseen and inscrutable forces, the organization can draw ever-increasing strength, vitality, and creativity from its people.

## 5. Educational strategy

OD seeks to stimulate organization self-renewal by changing behavior of people in the organization in significant ways through education. In this sense, however, education has little relationship to conventional in-service education concepts that are usually (a) chiefly concerned with the acquisition of cognitive knowledge (b) in a typical classroom setting that emphasizes the learner as a dependent recipient of knowledge.

OD educational strategy and processes focus primarily upon the elements important in shaping the organizational climate and culture of the organization: that complex web of dynamic organizational variables that so deeply influences the way that people feel about their role in the organization, the attitudes and expectations they develop toward their coworkers, and the quality of the relationships between individuals and groups within the organization. Conventionally, these kinds of problems—involving conflict, communication barriers, suspicion and fear, and questions of organizational effectiveness—have been skirted carefully in organizations: they are too "touchy," too sensitive to do much about. OD seeks to find ways not only to face such problems, which are central to the organization's functioning, but also to increase the participant's abilities to solve them in productive ways.

## 6. *Experienced behavior*

The concept of learning-by-doing applied to organizational life is the basis for learning in OD. Educative techniques strongly stress the building of knowledge and skill in organizational behavior through a two-step experience-based process in which a work-related group of people (1) share a common experience and then (2) examine that experience to see what they can learn from it.

This can be done in relatively controlled conditions of laboratory training, such as in a T-group. It can also be a study of real-life experiences that group members have actually shared in the organization. But the basis for learning is the group's actual experience, not some hypothetical situations. The group members are encouraged to question and to raise issues concerning group functioning, drawing insights and learning directly from this experience.

One purpose of this insistence upon examining one's experience in this way is to develop within the participants a long-lasting set of techniques and understandings that will enable them to learn and profit from their own experiences repeatedly over a sustained period of time. If this can be developed as a significant part of the group life of an organization, it can be a strong element of the desired self-renewal process.

## 7. *Dealing with real problems*

OD is applied to an organization in order to deal with existing, pressing problems. In some cases these problems may be serious enough to threaten the very survival of the organization, although they are usually not so dramatic. The educational processes do not involve learning about someone else's problem or discussing general cases but are directed to the specific organization under consideration—with its special conditions that make it unique.

What kind of problems might call for OD in a school? An attempt to catalogue such a wide range of possibilities would not be helpful, but the mention of a few typical situations might be useful:

1. Conditions of rapid change—such as a major school district reorganization or the result of a sweeping court order—might promote an "identity crisis" and organizational confusion of considerable magnitude.
2. A leadership crisis, such as the situation in which the new superintendent finds that there is little response to his initiatives.
3. Poor organizational effectiveness (however it is measured) that must be resolved in ways other than defensiveness or seeking excuses.
4. A high level of conflict, whether evidenced by excessive bickering and infighting or the apathy characteristic of withdrawal from too painful a situation.

Often, of course, these kinds of problems are interrelated; opening up one for examination and solution may well lead to other problems that were not considered to be of great concern at the outset. This heuristic characteristic of OD concepts and processes has great power to penetrate to the central problems of the organization. Therefore the major criterion in identifying the problem to be worked on in initial stages is that it be of genuine concern to the organization's participants—something they feel is important to them, rather than something only someone else is concerned about.

OD efforts should be viewed in the long-term sense suggested by the self-renewal concept, enabling the process to start from seemingly superficial problems and eventually reach the core. OD is not a one-shot approach to the alleviation of some limited, narrowly defined crisis after which it will be abandoned. Indeed, as OD techniques become more popular and respectable in the eyes of administrators and managers, there is rising concern that the demand for such a "band-aid" approach (identifying OD with management by crisis rather than the development of self-renewal) could discredit more ethical OD approaches.

## 8. *A planned strategy*

Another characteristic of OD—again in harmony with its overall systems approach—is that the effort must be planned systematically. The technology of OD embraces a wide range of possible activities and techniques. But they, in themselves, do not constitute OD. Indeed, a defining characteristic of OD is that it is a form of *planned change:* a strategy in which goals have been identified and a design for achieving them laid out. The plan must be specific: identifying target populations, establishing a timetable, and committing resources necessary to its fulfillment. The plan must also be tailored specifically to the particular circumstances of the organization.

Emphasizing the importance of a plan for OD should not imply rigidity. Indeed, if the effort is initially successful it is probable that the increasing involvement of participants will require modifying and shaping of the plan over time. It is important to provide for this in the planning stages, lest the effort turn into just another in-service program. Conversely, however, haphazard introduction of bits and pieces of OD technology without clear purposive planning and the commitment to carry it through can do more harm than good.

It has been noted, for example, that the decision to undertake OD in an organization can *in itself* produce some organizational improvement. This is not fully understood, and it may be merely a manifestation of the Hawthorne Effect.[5] However, the decision to undertake OD is often a ". . . signal to the members involved that the culture is changing, that new ideas and new ways of doing things are becoming more of a possibility and reality." [6] Obviously, a badly mounted OD program or the sudden termination of one (due, perhaps, to the administrator's timidity or lack of sufficient resources for the program) that has been started following the raising of hopes can result in an understandable backlash of feeling.

An OD program is a complex and sophisticated undertaking; it involves a wide range of possible interventions that deal with potentially sensitive matters. A highly qualified OD specialist can often facilitate the planning and carrying out of such a program by helping the administrator develop a practical OD design tailored to the specific realities of his organization. The designing of an OD project offers both administrator and behavioral scientist the rare opportunity to collaborate in common cause.

---

[5] The term *Hawthorne Effect* is generally used in behavioral science research in referring to the phenomenon that when experimental treatments are applied to groups (such as giving them new equipment or providing special attention) the groups tend to respond in positive ways. It is often a confounding variable in controlled experimental conditions. It can be used purposively, however, to produce *temporary* improvement in motivation and morale of work groups. See Robert G. Owens, *Organizational Behavior in Schools* (Englewood Cliffs, N.J.: Prentice-Hall, Inc., 1970), p. 10.

[6] Ibid., p. 102.

## 9. *Change agent*

OD is characterized by the participation of a change agent who has a vital and very specific role to play, at least in the initial stages of the change effort. Indeed, OD—in the various forms presently known to us—is impossible without a competent change agent. This person may have various official titles in different organizations; regardless, the term *consultant* is almost always used among OD practitioners to refer to the specialist who helps an organization design and carry out an OD program.

The consultant is so vital to the success or failure of OD that a substantial part of the literature is devoted to descriptions of his role, function, and specialized competencies, the nature of his relationships to client organizations, and so forth.

Finding an appropriate consultant and establishing an effective working relationship with him may well be the administrator's most crucial role in establishing OD in his school. Indeed, the need for consultant help has been the source of some of the thorniest problems in implementing OD. There can be much confusion, under the best of circumstances, about the consultant: what his role is, who he takes orders from, what impact his presence has upon the usual relationships between administrators and teachers—these are some of the problem-areas that commonly appear in OD work. They are the subject of considerable study and discussion among OD consultants themselves, as they attempt to shape their own roles in appropriate ways.

In general terms, consultants may be either from outside the organization (external consultants) or from within the organization (internal consultants). In its early history, OD efforts depended exclusively upon external consultants. Of course, the relationship of the external consultant to the organization is temporary and requires that extra money be found to cover the consulting fees. One reaction to this has been efforts to train individuals appropriately so that they may function as internal consultants; [7] typically, once such a position has been budgeted it tends to become a long-term "built in" arrangement. It appears likely that the role of internal change agents, or consultants, will become increasingly visible and formalized in school districts in the years ahead. However, the need for external consultants to deal with particularly complex and difficult problems of change will probably not be completely eliminated.

Some limited progress has been made in developing procedures for

[7] See, for example, Spencer Wyant, *Organizational Development from the Inside: A Progress Report on the First Cadre of Organizational Specialists* (Eugene, Oregon: Center for the Advanced Study of Educational Administration, 1972).

carrying out certain crucial aspects of OD activities without the direct assistance of behavioral science consultants.[8] At this stage of the development of OD, however, the consultant is a key individual. Policy and administration problems in dealing with OD consultants are discussed later in this book.

## 10. *Involvement of top-level administration*

Inevitably, one must conclude from the social systems orientation of OD that in order to change the organization we must deal with the entire system. The idea that we can change the functioning of part of the system in meaningful ways without affecting other parts of the system is simply untenable in the systems view. Organizational change is not a matter of "us" (the administration) changing "them" (the teachers and other subordinates) or even of changing "it" (the organization as some sort of entity detached from "us"). Administration must be very much an active partner involved in the development process to assure that all parts (i.e., subsystems) of the organizational system will stay appropriately linked together in the dynamic interactive way that is one of the identifying characteristics of the increasingly effective organization.

In operational terms, OD recognizes that organizations *are* hierarchical and will continue to be. When subordinates see that administration is doing something *to* organizations in the name of improving their effectiveness—something in which administrators are not involved except as observers—the subordinates are very likely to be wary and less than fully committed. On the other hand, if administration is already interested in the undertaking, committed to it, and involved in visible ways, subordinates are much more inclined to view the effort as valid and will be more highly motivated to involve themselves. In any organization, subordinates tend to develop highly sensitive antennae that pick up reliable indications of what is *really* important at higher levels through all the static and noise that may surround the issuance of official statements.

This was illustrated in the case of a large suburban school district. Located in a highly industrialized community, the district was undergoing the stresses and strains related to social and ethnic problems that have become so commonplace in recent years. The new superintendent—young, bright, articulate, energetic, with an enviable record in other districts—moved early to bring the principals and other key administrators together and organize them as a cabinet. With a new and greater opportunity to play a crucial role in establishing policy and dealing with

[8] Jack R. Gibb, "TORI Theory: Consultantless Team-building," *Journal of Contemporary Business*, I (Summer 1972): 33–43.

district-wide problems, this group was soon involved in important district-wide issues that had important implications for each school. Unfortunately, the cabinet soon ran into difficulties: wrangling broke out, decisions arrived at in meetings were undercut by private deals made outside of the cabinet (often involving school board members), and some members created an alliance to control voting on issues before the cabinet on the basis of the self-interest of their departments or schools. A number of principals—who had enjoyed considerable autonomy under the previous superintendent to "wheel and deal" with school board members in behalf of their individual schools—felt that the whole cabinet idea was simply a scheme to undermine them. The superintendent discussed these problems with the group and won easy agreement that a consultant should be brought in to help them find solutions.

The consultant was able to establish a basis for working with the group during an exploratory meeting. In addition to agreeing upon some goals and some modes of operating, certain ground rules were also agreed upon. One suggested by the consultant and quickly supported unanimously, was that all members of the group must attend each scheduled training session if at all possible. This was a highly capable and sophisticated group and, within a few meetings with the consultant, there was general feeling that real progress was being made and that the training effort should be continued. At the session following that decision, the superintendent announced that—due to the eruption of an unforeseen crisis—he would have to rush off soon after the group convened.

At the next session, he strongly endorsed the training effort and expressed keen interest in it but had to hurry off to another emergency. At the subsequent session, the same thing occurred; only this time three principals—after a decent interval—withdrew and hurried off to attend to "emergencies" at their schools. Needless to say, the superintendent's cabinet members realized that with the original crisis eased, the training program was no longer a high priority matter at the top and they responded accordingly.

## MECHANICAL AND ORGANIC SYSTEMS

OD is based upon some very clear and precise ideas about what organizations are and what they should be. It is virtually impossible to find an OD specialist who can maintain an evenhanded neutrality in this matter; there is a widely shared view among OD specialists that many of the traditional views about organizations that we have inherited are simply inappropriate to contemporary conditions. Improving the effectiveness of organizations requires reexamining a number of assumptions about organizations that have long held the respectability of truth in administrative thought.

Overwhelmingly, the central characteristics of school organizations are those of classical organization theory—decision-making is centralized, strong down-the-line authority expects obedience from subordinates, an individual worker is held accountable for his individual productivity, and there is strong emphasis upon hierarchical supervision to assure that delegated tasks are performed in accordance with standard operating procedures. Conflict within the organization is usually suppressed, often by labeling it as "bad" or denying that it exists. When conflict management *is* required, however, the process is to take the matter directly to a superordinate administrator for decision. On the other hand, warfare between conflicting factions—usually carried on covertly, using the organization's own rules and approved code of behavior to "get" the opposition—is frequently encountered.

Organizations that emphasize these characteristics are often labeled "bureaucratic" as a shorthand way of identifying their culture and distinguishing them from organizations having markedly different characteristics. However, many organizations often appear to have the same characteristics as classical organization but are not bureaucratic in the full technical sense of that term. Schools and school systems are generally examples; manifesting the organizational culture usually associated with classical organizational theory yet not fully meeting the definition of bureaucracies. Such organizations are more correctly characterized as *mechanical.*[9]

There is growing realization, however, that broad changes in western culture are making it increasingly difficult to base administrative practice on such a view. Bennis has identified twentieth-century conditions that virtually require a shift from the mechanical concept of organization:

1. The emergence of the human sciences, such as psychology and sociology, and their contribution to the understanding of man's complexity
2. Rising aspirations of individuals
3. The development of a humanistic-democratic ethos.[10]

These rapidly emerging conditions sharply limit the effectiveness of older concepts of organizational discipline and control and give rise to greater need for an organization's participants to be involved in their own destiny. Thus, loyalty to the organization takes on a new dimension.

---

[9] The term *mechanistic* is also used in the literature to identify this concept of organization.

[10] Warren G. Bennis, *Changing Organizations* (New York: McGraw-Hill Book Company, 1966), pp. 190–91.

Teachers seek new meaning and reward from their efforts, new ways of finding satisfaction from their work. They are no longer as willing to sit by, powerless, while higher authorities decide what is to be done and oblige them to comply.

*Organic* organizational systems differ from mechanical systems in a number of crucial ways. Basically, the organic view rejects the notion of the organization as a mechanical system in favor of its being a *living social system*—with all of the dynamic subsystems relationships implied. Confidence and trust between individuals and groups within the organization take on new importance. Interdependence between individuals and groups is recognized as fundamental, with sharing responsibilities and control instead of competing for dominance. Conflict is recognized as a legitimate phenomenon of organizational life, and it is dealt with openly and frankly as a problem to be solved. Lateral communication in the organization is fully as important as communication up and down the formal chain of command, so that coordination of effort becomes more of a mutual concern and less exclusively the province of hierarchical control. Leadership style emphasizes consultation and a concern for the *processes* by which decisions are made and ways people can become involved.

The official leader of the organic organization seeks to increase the involvement of other experts in appropriate decision-making processes. This process is characterized by activities and physical facilities designed to open up communication and participation. For example, an administrator will often arrange to hold conferences and meetings away from his office—on neutral territory more conducive to open discussion.

Overarching all of this, however, is the need for authenticity in developing the new organic results-oriented work culture in the organization. This requires a willingness to do more than play games with new trappings of administrative processes for image-building purposes; such a cynical approach can lead to frustration on a new order. One administrator, for example, seeking to co-opt the faculty so as to strengthen his hand in getting some changes in the system, established an elected committee of representatives to plan a reorganization of the system. This group worked over a period of two years, involving the faculty in drafting and discussing proposals in successive stages of development. Throughout the process, the administrator carefully projected a public image of low-key collegial participation in the various discussion and committee meetings.

Unseen by the faculty, however, were the occasions when the administrator would summon the committee chairman to his office and—after invoking secrecy—specify points that had to be changed and conditions that had to be met in the reorganization proposals because of some vague and unknown consequences that might befall unless the changes were made. In time, this masked conflict between what the administrator wanted and what the faculty wanted broke into the open as virtual warfare—long past the point of discussion and mutual problem-solving. The result was that the administrator finally imposed his reorganization on a thoroughly disgruntled faculty and a period of long-term "cold" warfare was initiated.

### Mechanical-Organic Continuum

Simplistically, the question may be raised: which is better, an organization with organic characteristics or one with mechanical characteristics? The answer must be based on at least two conditions.

First, it is most helpful to think of the mechanical-organic dimension as being a continuum rather than a dichotomy. In applying such descriptive terms to actual organizations it is unlikely that one would often find a "pure" form of either concept in practice. The terms are helpful, however, if they are conceptualized as identifying the opposite ends of a continuum along which a given organization might be classified. The classification itself requires restraint and care, too, because precise measures of the dimensions do not exist. Indeed, while the mechanical-organic concept is exceedingly useful to the administrator as a practical way of analyzing his situation and discussing it, it must be remembered that the concept is rather global.

Second, the comparative study of organizations quickly points up the likelihood that different conditions faced by organizations should be met by different kinds of organizational arrangements. Some organizations—such as most manufacturing plants—deal with relatively stable conditions and have rather clearly defined tasks. Others—such as schools—are experiencing conditions of rather rapid (if not volatile) change and have numerous, diffuse goals. The former (i.e., stable conditions and well-defined tasks) will be seen as more effective if they exhibit mechanical-type characteristics, while the latter (i.e., changing conditions and ill-defined goals) will be more effective within the organic mode.[11]

### Dimensions of Mechanical-Organic Continuum

Bennis has suggested six ways in which organic systems differ from mechanical systems.[12] These are, in effect, characteristics that all organi-

---

[11] John J. Morse and Jay W. Lorsch, "Beyond Theory Y," *Harvard Business Review*, 48 (May-June 1970): 61–68.

[12] Warren G. Bennis, *Organization Development: Its Nature, Origins, and Prospects* (Reading, Mass.: Addison-Wesley Publishing Company, 1969), p. 15.

| MECHANICAL SYSTEMS | | ORGANIC SYSTEMS | |
|---|---|---|---|
| 1. Exclusive individual emphasis | | Relationships between and within groups emphasized | 1. |
| 2. Authority–obedience relationships | | Mutual confidence and trust | 2. |
| 3. Delegated and divided responsibility rigidly adhered to | | Interdependence and shared responsibility | 3. |
| 4. Strict division of labor and hierarchical supervision | | Multigroup membership and responsibility | 4. |
| 5. Centralized decision-making | | Wide sharing of responsibility and control | 5. |
| 6. Conflict resolution through suppression, arbitration, and/or warfare | | Conflict resolution through bargaining or problem-solving | 6. |

**Figure 5-1**
Dimensions of mechanical and organic systems. Reprinted by special permission from *Organization Development: Its Nature, Origins, and Prospects,* by Warren G. Bennis. Addison-Wesley, Reading, Massachusetts. Copyright © 1969. All rights reserved.

zations possess in greater or less degree. In Figure 5-1, each dimension has been expressed as a possible continuum. A specific organization might be described as falling somewhere along the continuum for each dimension; the sum of such a description would yield a profile—however rough—of the extent to which the observer perceived the organization as either mechanical or organic.

French and Bell identified seven characteristics of what they call "mechanistic" kinds of organizations. These also have a dimensional quality, in that the characteristics are rarely completely absent from a given complex organization. Rather, organizations vary more in the degree to which they lean toward one end or the other of a continuum. Figure 5-2 describes these seven dimensions in summary form.

Clearly, the tendency of an organization toward either the mechanical or the organic mode is not merely a matter of chance. On one level, it can reflect deliberate choice based upon (1) the nature of the tasks that the organization is expected to perform, (2) the clarity and specificity of its goals, and (3) the degree of uncertainty and change that the organization confronts. On another level, it can also reflect the concepts that the administrators in the hierarchy hold about the nature of organizations with the resultant implications for administrative practice.

| MECHANICAL SYSTEMS | ORGANIC SYSTEMS |
|---|---|
| 1. Highly differentiated and specialized tasks with precise specification of rights, responsibilities, methods | Continuous reassessment of tasks and responsibilities through interaction of those involved with functional changes easy to arrange |
| 2. Coordination and control through hierarchical supervision | Coordination and control through network of those involved and concerned which is in frequent communication |
| 3. Communication with external environment controlled by top offices of hierarchy | Communication relatively extensive and open |
| 4. Strong downward-oriented line of command | Emphasis on lateral and diagonal consultation, advice, information giving, as source of coordination and control |
| 5. Insistence upon loyalty to organization and superiors | Emphasis on the task, goal achievement, and improvement of the organization |
| 6. High value on local knowledge and experience | High value on mission-oriented expertness, cosmopolitan knowledge of the profession |
| 7. One-to-one leadership style | Team leadership style |

**Figure 5-2**
Dimensions of mechanical and organic systems. Based on Wendell L. French and Cecil H. Bell, Jr., *Organization Development* (Englewood Cliffs, N.J.: Prentice-Hall, Inc., 1973), pp. 183–85.

Those administrators who are deeply imbued with classical concepts of organization and administration will emphasize the chain of command, the importance of clearly specifying the operational "territory" of various offices and subunits, and will especially value those people who "know how things are done here." Such administrators usually will clearly reveal their orientation through their own administrative style. For example, such administrators would predictably favor the one-to-one administrative relationships depicted in Figure 5-3.

Administrators convinced of the practical value that organic views of the organization have to offer, tend to exhibit a rather different administrative style. As Figure 5-4 suggests, they tend to utilize a highly consultative, administrative team approach, encouraging open and free interaction among all of the team members. They emphasize consultation with other team members, sharing information, keeping others informed, seeking advice. The goal—as in the development of many another team—is to operate in such a way that decisions can be reached through group consensus. This not only suggests the absence of unilateral

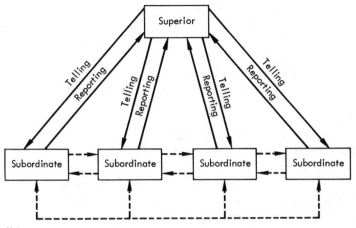

**Figure 5-3**
The one-to-one administrative style characteristic of the mechanical organizational system. Based on French and Bell, *Organizational Development,* p. 184.

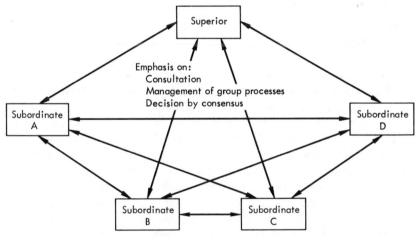

**Figure 5-4**
The administrative team style characteristic of the organic organizational system. Based on French and Bell, *Organization Development,* p. 186

decision by directives or the compromises and voting characteristic of parliamentary-type decision-making: it suggests a commonly shared agreement of the group in which everyone shares—no bargaining, no voting, no one-man decisions.

*A central thrust of organization development, then, is to move the system with mechanical characteristics in the direction of more organic characteristics. The aim is to improve the task achievement of the organizational system by improving the processes that the organization uses in making important decisions. To accomplish this, OD processes are focused primarily on the development of a highly task-oriented organizational climate and work culture that will actively and meaningfully involve participants in the key elements of the administrative process.*

## MOTIVATION AND LEADERSHIP IN ORGANIZATIONAL CHANGE

In administering change, it becomes the task of the administrator to provide leadership that will develop a climate in the organization that will permit—indeed, encourage—change to occur.

Leadership, by definition, takes place in a group: it obviously requires some human interaction and cannot be exercised in isolation. One of the basic concerns of leaders, then, is the motivation of people. What is it that causes people to join an organization, stay in it, and work toward its goals?

### Motivation

A fundamental, perhaps inevitable, conflict exists between the individual and the organization. Each individual has needs, wants, desires that he seeks to fulfill and satisfy. As a participant in an organization he has opportunity to meet some of his needs. The organization, on the other hand, places demands upon the individual. It would be a rare situation if one's job fully met his needs and satisfied the organization's demands upon him at the same time. Using social system concepts to visualize this, we can see that the behavior that one exhibits at work is the product of the interplay of individual needs on the one hand and demands of the organization on the other hand, as illustrated in Figure 5-5. Thus, there is inevitable tension and conflict between the individual and the organization.

The intensity of this conflict varies from organization to organization and person to person. The individual does, of course, seek to have his needs met; he will resist organizational demands that interfere with his own felt needs. The degree to which he resists depends largely upon the extent to which he *perceives* the organization as threatening the fulfillment of his needs. He will involve himself, on the other hand, in those organizational demands that he perceives to be concurrent with his own needs. While it is unlikely that the needs-demand relationship will often be identical, it can be controlled to considerable extent by management

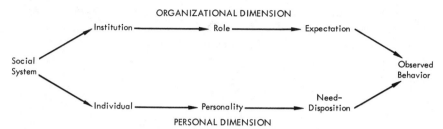

**Figure 5-5**
Organizational behavior is the product of interplay between individual needs and organizational demands. Jacob W. Getzels, "Administration as a Social Process," in Andrew W. Halpin, ed., *Administrative Theory in Education* (Chicago: Midwest Administration Center, U. of Chicago, 1958), p. 156.

of organizational demands in relationship to the motivations of participants.

Clearly, the job-performance of an individual (or work group) is strongly influenced by (1) his ability to do the job and (2) the motivation he has to do the work. William James, of Harvard, found that some employees could hold down jobs without being fired by merely working at about twenty or thirty percent of their ability. On the other hand, highly motivated employees will work closer to eighty to ninety percent of their ability. While these percentages will vary in specific situations, it is clear that the administrator seeking results-oriented organization development must give early and serious attention to his responsibility for motivating people in the organization to perform their work in the most productive way possible.

Classical approaches to motivation in administration link the worker's productivity to the size of his paycheck. Threat of dismissal is the ultimate negative expression of such a view, whereas increasing the worker's income is a positive expression of the concept. Much of the contemporary thrust to tie the job-security and income of teachers to so-called "productivity" is based upon this classical view.

In our contemporary affluent society, however, in which the teacher's fear of authoritarian power is much less potent than in earlier years of this century and authoritarian control increasingly resisted, administrators have less power to bend subordinates to the demands of the organization. There is, in fact, substantial reason to anticipate that insistence on resorting to a "tough" classical approach to motivation in schools will actually diminish productivity. However, new and powerful concepts of motivation—attuned to the realities of our time—are emerging. Properly understood and used by administrators they can be useful not merely for the short-run purpose of shoring up organizational performance but also to facilitate the concepts of OD in the schools.

Three highly compatible views of motivation—all developed since 1950—are generally held as basic to OD and to the contemporary practice of administration. They are (1) McGregor's Theory X and Theory Y, (2) Maslow's hierarchy of needs theory, and (3) Herzberg's motivation-hygiene theory.

## Theory X and Theory Y

Douglas McGregor was one of the pioneers of what is now known as organization development. His landmark book, *The Human Side of Enterprise*, has had wide impact upon business administration.

In the 1950's, while working at Union Carbide, McGregor produced two statements (or theories) which he felt explained certain aspects of the nature of man which underlies the thinking (hence, the actions) of administrators.

1. Theory X [13] postulates three basic propositions:

   a. The average human being has an inherent dislike for work and will avoid it if he can.
   b. Because of this characteristic, most people must be coerced, controlled, directed, and threatened with punishment so that they will work toward the organization's goals.
   c. The average human being prefers to be directed, wants security, and avoids responsibility.

Undoubtedly, many administrators share these views, believe them to be true, and act accordingly in their professional practice. Close, detailed supervision, the use of organizational power to motivate people, and the exercise of strong hierarchical control are often seen as essential to administrative practice.

2. Theory Y takes a different view:

   a. Physical work and mental work are as natural as play, if they are satisfying.
   b. Man will exercise self-direction and self-control toward an organization's goals if he is committed to them.
   c. Commitment is a function of rewards. The best rewards are satisfaction of ego and self-actualization.
   d. The average person can learn to accept and seek responsibility. Avoidance of it and emphasis on security are learned and are not inherent characteristics.

[13] This discussion of Theory X and Theory Y is drawn from Douglas M. McGregor, *The Human Side of Enterprise* (New York: McGraw-Hill Book Company, 1960), pp. 33–57.

e. Creativity, ingenuity, and imagination are widespread among people and do not occur only in a select few.

Obviously, administrators who feel that Theory Y offers a better explanation of man's nature will tend to differ markedly in their administrative practice from those who favor Theory X. One would expect them to lean discernably toward an organic view of organization. Such administrators are often handicapped in their administrative practice by the fact that conventionally organizational norms have been based primarily on Theory X. For that reason few administrators have been equipped by either experience or their graduate school training programs with specific skills for implementing Theory Y on a practical basis. OD offers opportunities to develop such specific skills and reorient the organization toward Theory Y beliefs.

*The hierarchy of needs theory*

Abraham Maslow, clearly one of this century's seminal thinkers in psychology, has developed an insight into motivation that has had profound impact upon administrative thought in the United States.

Maslow identified a number of needs that are important to most people; [14] these can be classified under five headings:

1. *Physiological needs*—basic human needs, such as food, clothing, and shelter.
2. *Security*—the need to be free of physical danger or the danger of being deprived of ways to meet the basic physiological needs.
3. *Social (or affiliative) needs*—the need to be accepted by other human beings, to "belong" and to have the approval of others.
4. *Esteem*—the need to be recognized by others through the granting of status, prestige, and power.
5. *Self-actualization*—the need to fulfill one's potential, or to do what one believes is important from his own point of view.

These needs—that provide the motivational force causing people to join an organization and work toward its goals—are actually experienced by individuals as a hierarchy of needs. Physiological necessities are the primary order of need in the hierarchy. Only after this basic need has been met reasonably well does the next higher level of need develop enough to motivate the individual. Although an individual may well be motivated by a number of needs, one will be predominant at a given

[14] A. H. Maslow, *Motivation & Personality* (New York: Harper & Row, Publishers, 1954).

time. Further, new needs emerge to motivate the individual only after lower-order needs have been satisfied.

The lowest order of human needs consists of the basic physiological necessities such as food, water, and shelter. In less complex societies of the past it was possible for one to meet these needs individually or as a participant in relatively primitive organizations. The nomadic hunter or the peasant in a simple agrarian society spent much of his time and energy providing these necessities for himself. In our modern technologically oriented society, however, it is not possible for many of us to dig a well for water or hunt for game when we are hungry. Rather, we must earn money to pay for such necessities as the rent, food, and taxes.

In modern society, the basic drives of human existence cause us to become enmeshed in organizational life—we become participants in the organization that employs us as well as the myriad government agencies and private companies that provide us with essential goods and services. Thus, at the simplest level of human need we are motivated to join organizations, remain in them, and contribute to their objectives.

However, because of the nature of man, once these needs are adequately met a new level of need that is one step higher in the hierarchy of needs automatically appears: the need for safety or security. This need, according to Maslow, now has the greater potency and the individual will seek to satisfy it. Security can, of course, mean many things to different people in different circumstances. For some, it means earning a high income to assure freedom from want in case of sickness or the onset of old age. Thus, many people are motivated to work harder to seek success, frequently measured in terms of income. Or security can be interpreted in terms of job security, so important, for example, to many civil service employees and school teachers. To them, the assurance of life tenure and a guaranteed pension may be strong motivating factors in their participation in employing organizations.

Street gangs, that often have a well-developed organizational structure, are commonly joined for the safety they offer their members in a threatening environment. Often a gang or coalition of gangs will take over a school and terrorize nonmembers into joining the gang or leaving the school. Some urban youths leave school because they cannot find an organization that will meet their needs for safety, rather than because they dislike studying.

New levels of need unfold as the needs below them are met. Once the need for safety is satisfied, the individual is free to try to meet his normal need for love and affiliation. Until the earlier needs are met, however—the basic physiological needs and the need for safety or security—the individual will be motivated by them more highly than by any psychological need. Thus, a man who is out of work and growing short of funds would probably find the promise of high pay a good reason for taking a job with a particular company. However, once the individual has enough income to get along reasonably well, he can begin to think in terms of his security. And once he achieves security, the employee with a reasonably well-paying and solid job will begin to feel the need of belonging and approval. He will not only become aware of these needs, but will also try to find situations in which they can be met; moreover, he will tend to behave in a way intended to produce the response that will best meet this need for love and affiliation.

Higher levels in the hierarchy of needs described by Maslow are the need for esteem, next, the need for knowledge and understanding and, finally, the need to attain self-actualization. The latter is the highest order of need in the Maslow formulation and represents the need for personal fulfillment. Thus, higher needs emerge in a relatively orderly and predictable manner as lower needs are satisfied.[15] (See Figure 5-6.)

*Motivation-hygiene theory*

Frederick Herzberg collected a great deal of data about the attitudes and feelings of people toward their jobs, through extensive interviewing of

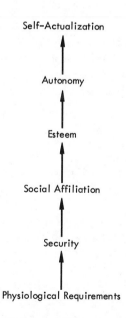

**Figure 5-6**
A hierarchy of human needs related to motivation.

[15] This discussion of Maslow's theory is from Robert G. Owens, *Organizational Behavior in Schools* (Englewood Cliffs, N.J.: Prentice-Hall, Inc., 1970), pp. 30–31.

a wide range of employees in business and industrial firms, ranging from hourly workers to engineers, accountants, and researchers to top-level administrators. In analyzing these data, Herzberg discovered that the needs of people on the job seem to fall into two distinct categories. In general, when people are dissatisfied with their jobs their concern primarily centers about the environment in which they work: the atmosphere in the place, its work culture, its organizational climate. On the other hand, when people are satisfied with their jobs they tend to be less concerned with environmental factors and are more concerned about the work itself.

Many factors combine to create the environment in which people work; indeed, the field of organizational climate has drawn considerable attention from scholars trying to unravel the complexities involved. Herzberg, however, emphasized five factors that are experienced directly by workers:

1. Organizational policies and administration
2. Supervision
3. Working conditions
4. Interpersonal relations
5. Money, status, and security

These so-called *hygiene factors* do not motivate people to do better work. However, when they are causes of worker dissatisfaction they can also cause reduced effort and productivity. In a sense, a work environment *seen by the worker* as satisfactory is a basic foundation that must exist before problems of motivation can be seriously considered.

The factors that motivate people are directly involved with the work itself:

1. The sense of achievement
2. The recognition received for accomplishments
3. The challenge the work offers
4. The responsibility the work carries
5. The feeling of growth and development that comes from doing the work.

These, according to Herzberg's widely used analysis, are *motivators:* these are the principal factors that develop the kind of job satisfaction that tends to increase the quality of performance.

As an illustration of the motivation-hygiene theory in practice, we might take the hypothetical case of a fourth-grade teacher who has a long-standing reputation for being an excellent, hard-working teacher. Because she is such an excellent teacher the principal routinely has recognized her professional status in his supervisory activities. Suppose that, as a result of a new policy, a new assistant principal is assigned to the school for the purpose of stepping up supervision.

**Table 5-1.** *Factors in motivation-hygiene theory.*

| Hygiene Factors | Motivating Factors |
|---|---|
| Environment | The Job Itself |
| Policies and administration | Achievement |
| Supervision | Recognition for accomplishment |
| Working conditions | Challenging work |
| Interpersonal relationships | Increased responsibility |
| Money, status, security | Growth and development |

Based on Paul Hersey and Kenneth H. Blanchard, *Management of Organizational Behavior*, second edition (Englewood Cliffs, N.J.: Prentice-Hall, Inc., 1969), p. 55.

It turns out that the new AP—a young man perhaps, whom the teacher feels is less qualified than she, even though he has higher position and higher salary—proceeds to administer a new and more rigorous supervisory program that the teacher finds demeaning, if not foolish. The teacher's ability would, of course, remain unchanged; the policies and the supervision under which she worked, however, would be very much changed.

Since we know that performance on the job (or productivity) involves motivation as well as ability, the unsatisfied hygiene need (i.e., supervision that is "acceptable") would probably lead to reduced performance. This might not be at all intentional on the part of the teacher: it could simply be an unconscious reaction to perceived harrassment, embarrassment, and loss of confidence in the system. In the motivation-hygiene concept, it would be unrealistic to expect that teacher to feel again the same involvement and motivation from her work as long as the hygiene dissatisfaction remained. Further, following such an incident, it would be very difficult to restore the original level of productivity by restoring the hygiene factors to their previous levels; and increasing the teacher's productivity beyond the original levels that had been normal for her would be virtually impossible. (Figure 5-7).

### Job enrichment

The three approaches to motivation discussed here—Theory X and Theory Y, the hierarchy of needs theory, and motivation-hygiene theory—are not only compatible but highly complementary in providing the administrator with insights that are useful in developing a self-renewing organization. One of the key administrative concepts that has emerged from these views of human motivation is that of job enrichment.

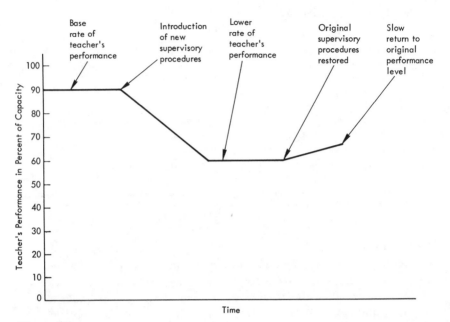

**Figure 5-7**
An illustration of the effect of hygiene dissatisfiers on a teacher's performance over time.

Basically, job enrichment—acknowledging that performance is a function of ability and motivation—takes the view that one's ability is not fixed: it can, in many cases, be increased through the use of appropriate motivational techniques. For example, take the case of a teacher who likes his work and does well at it. Perhaps, as shown in Figure 5-7, he may be said to be working at ninety percent of his performance capability: obviously, such a person must be getting a high degree of motivation from the work itself—feelings of pride, reward, satisfaction, and doing what he wants to do. There seems to be little else that can be done to increase such a teacher's productivity.

However, if such a teacher can be placed in an opportunity where he exercises greater responsibility, has more freedom to use his initiative and creativity, to exercise some leadership in making decisions and handling problems—in other words to meet some of his more mature motivational needs—*he will probably grow with the job*. With renewed interest and increased feelings of confidence and self-direction he will tend to set new goals, new performance levels for himself. Thus, by enriching job experience, it is possible not only to get better-satisfied workers, but also to actually increase their performance levels. (See Figure 5-8)

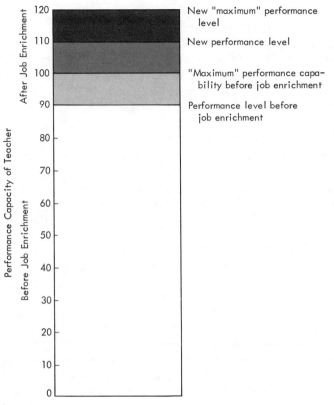

**Figure 5-8**
In job enrichment, satisfying motivators have the effect of increasing job performance capability over the previous "maximum."

### Anatomy of Leadership

Traditionally, the nature of leadership has been examined on the basis of certain inborn traits that leaders presumably have. The concept rests upon the conviction that certain individuals—unlike the rest of the population—are born possessing the traits requisite for leadership; and it is important to identify those individuals as early in life as possible and help them, so that they may exercise their special capabilities. Extensive research has failed to support this concept.

Although there have been numerous attempts to identify the human traits that are necessary for effective leadership, it seems unlikely that a general description of such traits is possible. There are too many different successful leadership styles and techniques to support the "trait theory".

Leadership is a highly dynamic relationship between an individual and other members of a group in a specific environment. What counts is not so much the traits that the leader may or may not possess as it is the kinds of things he *does*. The focus, therefore, is not so much upon the generalized effect of the leader-group relationship (that is called leadership) as it is upon the way in which the leader exercises his influence (that is leader behavior). *It is through the analysis of leader behavior that we can hope to identify the elements of leadership that can be studied, learned, and practiced.*

In general, leadership may be viewed as a process: a process in which others are influenced to act to achieve goals in a specific situation. Thus, the important elements of leadership are (1) the behavior of the leader, (2) the behavior of the followers, and (3) the environment of the situation.

Although there is a wide range of possible leader behavior style, for the purpose of simplifying the discussion the choice can be thought of in polarized terms:

1. The leader can decide what to do and tell his followers how to do it.
2. The leader permits his followers to operate freely within limits dictated by things over which he has no control.

Obviously, the authoritarian leader (the one who decides and tells) has a Theory X orientation toward his followers, whereas the democratic leader (the one who permits followers to operate freely) places his reliance in Theory Y. Oversimplified, these two leadership styles can be differentiated as being either *task oriented* or *people oriented*. Figure 5-9 gives some indication of the range of leadership styles that lies between these polar positions.

Leadership style evidenced by a specific leader is a combination between task-oriented behavior and people-oriented behavior. Some leaders are very task-oriented, whereas others are much more concerned for human relationships. Most leaders show a balance of behavior somewhere in between. These *two dimensions of leadership* have been identified time and time again in research on leader behavior. According to Dorwin Cartwright and Alvin Zander, *one dimension is concerned with the achievement of some specific group goal and the other is concerned with the maintenance or strengthening of the group itself.*[16] Daniel Katz referred to the dimensions of leadership as *employee orientation* and *production orientation.*[17] Likert used the terms *employee-centered* to describe

---

[16] Dorwin Cartwright & Alvin Zander, eds., *Group Dynamics: Research & Theory*, 2nd ed. (Evanston, Il.: Row, Peterson & Company, 1960).
[17] Daniel Katz, N. Maccoby, and Nancy C. Morse, *Productivity, Supervision and Morale in an Office Situation* (Ann Arbor, Mich.: Survey Research Center, University of Michigan, 1950).

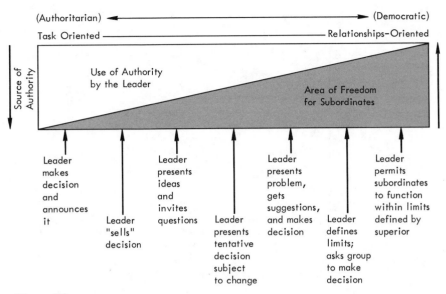

**Figure 5-9**
Leadership style is evident in a range of possible behaviors. From Paul Hersey and Kenneth H. Blanchard, *Management of Organizational Behavior: Utilizing Human Resources* (Prentice-Hall, Inc., 1972), p. 71. Adapted from Robert Tannenbaum and Warren H. Schmidt, "How to Choose a Leadership Pattern," *Harvard Business Review*, March-April 1958.

the attention given to the human aspects of group members and *job-centered* in referring to the emphasis placed on production.[18] The Ohio State Leadership Studies, begun by the Bureau of Business Research in 1945, called them *initiating structure* and *consideration*.[19] Andrew Halpin used these dimensions to analyze the leader behavior of school superintendents and described them thus:

1. *Initiating structure* refers to the leader's behavior in delineating the relationship between himself and the members of his work group, and in endeavoring to establish well-defined patterns of organization, channels of communication, and methods of procedure.

2. *Consideration* refers to behavior indicative of friendship, mutual trust, respect, and warmth in the relationship between the leader and the members of his staff.[20]

[18] Rensis Likert, *New Patterns of Management* (New York: McGraw-Hill Book Company, 1961), p. 7.
[19] *Leader Behavior Description Questionnaire-Form XII*, Copyright © 1962 by the Bureau of Business Research, College of Commerce and Administration, The Ohio State University, Columbus, Ohio.
[20] Andrew W. Halpin, *Theory and Research in Administration* (New York: The Macmillan Company, 1966), p. 86.

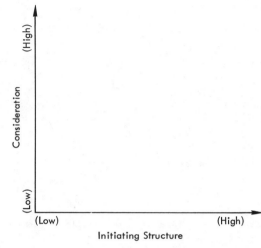
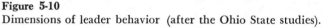

**Figure 5-10**
Dimensions of leader behavior (after the Ohio State studies).

## Grid concepts of leadership

If there are two dimensions of leader behavior, the performance of a specific leader must be viewed as embracing both dimensions—but not necessarily equally. In terms of observed behavior, then, *initiating structure* and *consideration* may be depicted as in Figure 5-10. Actually, however, the range of leader behavior styles tends to cluster around four principal quadrants of a grid pattern, as shown in Figure 5-11.

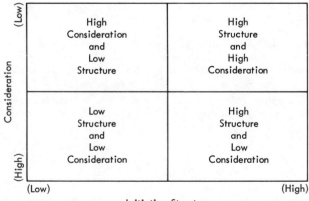

**Figure 5-11**
The Ohio State leadership quadrants.

Many research studies have been conducted using this concept for categorizing leader behavior according to the two-dimensional *initiating structure/consideration* construct. Although many of these studies have been conducted in business and industrial firms, other organizations— such as the military and public education—have also been studied. If the judgment of both superordinates and subordinates is indicative of the effectiveness of leaders, the gist of this research is clear: those leaders who evidence behavior that is high both in initiating structure and in consideration are generally viewed as effective leaders, as opposed to those who project another "mix" of the two behavioral dimensions.

The Managerial Grid®, developed by Blake and Mouton,[21] has been popular in clarifying the dynamics of the dimensions of organizational leadership. Its use is helpful in identifying the alternatives available to an administrator in improving his effectiveness as a leader. The Grid is sometimes used as the basis for initiating organization development work in an organization because it helps to focus directly upon critical elements of organizational culture.

The Grid has two axes: one indicates *concern for people* and the other *concern for production* (Figure 5-12). For the administrator, these

Concern for Production

**Figure 5-12**
The two axes of the Managerial Grid represent the interaction of two concerns of the leader.

[21] Robert R. Blake and Jane Srygley Mouton, *The Managerial Grid* (Austin, Texas: Scientific Methods, Inc., 1964).

THE MANAGERIAL GRID

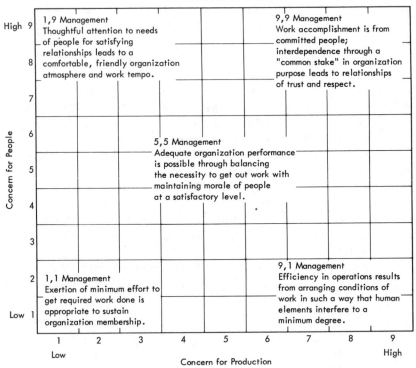

**Figure 5-13**
The Managerial Grid figure ®. From *The Managerial Grid,* by Robert R. Blake and Jane Srygley Mouton. Houston: Gulf Publishing Company, 1964, p. 10. Reproduced by permission.

two concerns do not remain isolated but interact with one another as he works with others. This interaction of his concern for people and his concern for production (e.g., achievement of the organization's goals) very much influences his thinking, his actions, and his feelings in the course of his work.

Figure 5-13 shows the complete Managerial Grid. Five patterns stand out as those most commonly used by administrators:

> *1, 1 pattern* (lower left of The Grid) is that of the administrator who is "going through the motions." Because essentially he has little concern for either people or production, he is not really involved in the organization's affairs and contributes little to them.
>
> *9, 1 pattern* (lower right of The Grid) depicts the administrator with (a) little concern for his subordinates or other people in the organization but (b) intense concern for getting things done. In all likelihood he

knows what has to be done and directs subordinates toward his goals.

*5, 5 pattern* (in the center of The Grid) is that of the person (a) moderately concerned with production and (b) also somewhat concerned with maintaining a reasonable level of morale. By sticking to the middle of the road he keeps the organization stable and "average."

*1, 9 pattern* (upper left) is that of a leader who probably believes that a happy group will be productive. Therefore, he is little concerned with production directly and devotes much attention to maintaining satisfying relationships in the group.

*9, 9 pattern* (upper right) strongly reflects McGregor's Theory Y orientation: people can be highly involved and enjoy their work, the demands of production can coincide nicely with the needs that people have for satisfaction and recognition from their work.

These five patterns represent distinctive leadership styles. Part of the popularity of the Blake-Mouton Managerial Grid rests upon the articulate and explicit way in which the various leadership styles are described. This has been helpful to the practitioner who is concerned with the practicality of Grid concepts rather than their theoretical niceties. In discussing Grid concepts, for example, Blake and his associates have described the major Grid styles thus:

*(1, 1) Impoverished*—exertion of minimum effort to get required work done is barely sufficient to sustain organization membership.

*(9, 1) Task*—efficiency in operations results from arranging conditions of work in such a way that human elements interfere to a minimum degree.

*(5, 5) Middle of the Road*—adequate organization performance is possible through balancing the necessity to get work done, while maintaining morale of people at a satisfactory level.

*(1, 9) Country Club*—thoughtful attention to the needs of people for satisfying relationships leads to comfortable friendly organization atmosphere and work tempo.

*(9, 9) Team*—work accomplishment is from committed people; interdependence through a "common stake" in organization purpose leads to relationships of trust and respect.[22]

Blake and Mouton have made it clear that in their view the 9, 9 pattern (the team approach) of leadership is likely to yield optimum results in most organizations. In fact, an extensive training program aimed at helping corporation executives and managers to shift their styles in this direction has been conducted in many nations of the world.

Clearly, then, leader behavior tends to cluster around the two dimensions described above. Numerous students of organizations have dis-

[22] Robert R. Blake, et al., "Breakthrough in Organization Development," *Harvard Business Review* (November-December 1964), p. 136.

covered this and have variously named and described the dimensions. Of all the attempts to identify these dimensions, the Blake/Mouton formulation is probably of most practical use, partly because it is most explicit. Thus, we are enabled to identify and discuss organizational leadership in relatively clear and unambiguous terms. We are also able to conceptualize the possibilities of deliberately shifting leader behavior style from some present form to a potentially more effective style—and, in the same vein, move the organization from its present level of effectiveness to new and higher levels.

*Authenticity and skill*

Leader behavior has thus far been discussed in conceptual and theoretical terms. This is necessary in attempting to understand practical situations and problems at the cognitive level. At the action level, however, leader behavior is shaped not merely by our "knowledge" but also by our beliefs, values, and feelings. To be effective, the leader's behavior must be authentic: a genuine expression of his views, values, beliefs. Inauthentic behavior—the superficial gesture in deference to popular opinion—is soon spotted as phony and has a negative impact upon others in the group. "Spraygun consideration," as Halpin called it—typified by "the P.T.A. smile, and by the oily affability dispensed by administrators at faculty picincs and office parties" [23]—is hardly likely to be accepted by subordinates as anything else. Authentic behavior, on the other hand, that reflects genuine inner beliefs, is likely to be recognized for what it is.

While some may cling to a stereotype of school administrators as individuals who are primarily concerned about bureaucratic concepts of organizational structure and hardly concerned about the human dimension of administration, there is little evidence to support the view. In fact, we find that if one applies Grid concepts in either preservice or in-service training programs in educational administration, the participants generally reveal a remarkably high orientation to the human dimension of organizational behavior. We find little reason to challenge the belief that educational administrators in the United States today are highly committed to humanistic values and that they are reasonably well-versed in behavioral concepts of leadership. The commonly observed discrepancy between these values and administrative practice appears to reflect the difficulties inherent in translating them into effective patterns of administrative behavior. The problem is not that educational administrators have been oversold on the desirability of a humanistic point of view but, rather, that the techniques and skills for implementing the point of view in practice has been only partially integrated in the pro-

---

[23] Halpin, *Theory and Research in Administration,* p. 86.

grams of study that have prepared them for professional practice. Our experience is that practicing administrators are well aware of this and eagerly seek opportunities to improve and develop specific skills in integrating both the task and human dimensions of leadership.

A number of OD-related techniques have been developed to help individuals acquire these skills through action research in group situations.[24] These provide the leader opportunities to assess the impact of his behavior on others, to develop and experiment with possibly more effective behaviors, and to practice them in group situations. They also provide opportunities for others in the organizational group to develop more productive modes of behavior in response. The resulting change in group performance can encourage the development of an ongoing *process* of self-renewal in the school.

The experience of the High School Self-Renewal Program of the Economic Development Council of New York City exemplifies this approach. Their research and experience indicate that high schools are not likely to solve their problems until each school has developed an ongoing process designed to facilitate its own organizational self-renewal. This process is viewed as "a stream of interconnected actions and events that seems to lend itself to complex planning efforts in schools. The process employs numerous Organization Development techniques, including problem identification and analysis, goal-setting, priorities selection, definition of objectives, reallocation of resources and, finally, action planning, institutional change, and evaluation of results." [25] A central thrust of the process implies a clear role for the school administrator: one that stresses the need to facilitate wide participation in the process. This role calls upon the administrator to provide leader behavior that will tend to move the school toward a more organic mode emphasizing the importance of effective involvement of faculty, community, and other appropriate groups in identifying and solving problems. Clearly, leader behavior that emphasizes and reinforces the more mechanistic concepts of organization and leadership tends to be dysfunctional under such circumstances.

## SUMMARY

Organization Development (OD) is emerging as a major strategy of organizational change, applying theory and technology of behavioral science

---

[24] See, for example, Richard A. Schmuck, and Philip J. Runkel, et al., *Handbook of Organization Development in Schools* (Palo Alto: National Press Books, 1972).
[25] "Participative Planning in Inner-City High Schools" (draft document, New York: Economic Development Council of New York City, September 1, 1974), p. 3.

to the improvement of problem-solving and self-renewal processes of organizations. Ten central concepts of OD are:

1. The goal is improved functioning of the organization.
2. The organization is a complex sociotechnical system.
3. Organizations can develop self-renewing characteristics.
4. The focus of organizational change efforts is on people.
5. It is a normative-reeducative approach.
6. The basis for learning in OD is experienced behavior.
7. Learning for OD takes place while confronting real organizational problems.
8. Organizational change requires a long-term planned approach.
9. A change agent/consultant plays an essential role in planned organizational change.
10. Top-level administration must be actively involved.

In general terms, the essential thrust of OD is to shift an organization and its administration from a mechanical orientation to a more organic orientation. Such a shift is a challenge to traditional administrative thought and practice, especially with regard to the exercise of the human skills involved in motivating and leading subordinates.

Organization development concepts of motivation tend to represent a synthesis that draws heavily from (1) McGregor's *Theory X and Theory Y*, (2) Maslow's *hierarchy of prepotent needs* theory, and (3) Herzberg's *motivation-hygiene* theory.

Effective leadership is crucial to achieving the more effective organizational performance that is the goal of OD. Although in the past there has been little knowledge about leadership and how it may be more effectively exercised, research since the 1950s has shown that leader behavior is strongly influenced by two key dimensions: (1) concern for production and (2) concern for people. OD theory and technology enable administrators to learn to redirect their leader behavior into more effective patterns, using these dimensions.

Organization Development and administrative style are each based upon explicit concepts of organizational theory and leadership. In schools where the administrator's behavior is largely shaped by Theory X views, the chances of significant OD success are minimal; where the administrator's style of leadership more nearly conforms to Theory Y concepts, however, OD may be very helpful. OD offers little promise of significant change to the organization being led by an administrator with a 9, 1 orientation. It offers a great deal of specific help to the administrator who leans toward a 9, 9 orientation and seeks specific ways to implement those views throughout the organization.[26]

Administrators who are interested in stimulating organizational change through OD, therefore, need to examine thoughtfully the beliefs and values that govern their practice. OD requires considerable administrative support and involvement, and not just a little change on the part of the administrator himself. Unless the administrator has already developed an authentic commitment to at least the theoretical rationale underlying OD, he might be wise to develop his own administrative style before plunging the school into an OD project.

## SUGGESTED READING

BENNIS, WARREN G. *Organization Development: Its Nature, Origins, and Prospects.* Reading, Massachusetts: Addison-Wesley Publishing Company, 1969. Chapter 1. An easy-to-read nontechnical description of OD. Deals not only with conceptual bases but provides some concrete operational illustrations. This little book is an OD classic and is one of the widely respected Addison-Wesley "six-pack" of paperbacks on OD.

BUCHANAN, PAUL C. "The Concept of Organization Development or Self-Renewal, as a Form of Planned Change." In *Concepts for Social Change,* ed. by Goodwin Watson. Washington, D.C.: National Training Laboratories, NEA, 1967. This eight-page essay describes organization development and explains the general concepts upon which it is based. *Concepts for Social Change* and *Change in School Systems,* both edited by Goodwin Watson, are two small paperbacks that elucidate the theoretical and conceptual basis for the Cooperative Project for Educational Development (COPED).

HERSEY, PAUL and BLANCHARD, KENNETH H. *Management of Organizational Behavior.* 2nd ed. Englewood Cliffs, N.J.: Prentice-Hall, Inc., 1969. For a lucid description of contemporary behavioral views of important elements of administrative style see especially Chapter 1: "Management: a Behavioral Approach"; Chapter 2: "Motivation and Behavior"; Chapter 3: "Motivating Environment"; and Chapter 4: "Leader Behavior."

MOUTON, JANE SRYGLEY and BLAKE, ROBERT R. "Behavioral Science Theories Underlying Organization Development." *Journal of Contemporary Business* 1 (Summer 1972): 9–22. The Managerial Grid approach to OD has been little used in American public schools but is extensively utilized in business, industry, and public administration around the world. In this article the authors of The Grid explain how OD and administrative style are (1) closely related, (2) based upon behavioral science theories, and (3) interpreted by Grid concepts.

[26] There appear to be some organizational conditions that forecast the likelihood of success or failure of an OD effort in schools. These appear to be closely related to the leadership style in the school. See, for example, Steven L. Saturen, "On the Way to Adaptability: Some Conditions for Organizational Self-Renewal in Elementary Schools." (Ph.D. diss., University of Oregon, 1972).

SCHMUCK, RICHARD A., and MILES, MATTHEW B. *Organization Development in Schools.* Palo Alto: National Press Books, 1971. Chapter 1. The authors are clearly in the vanguard of applying OD to schools. In this tightly compressed twenty-three-page chapter they provide an elegant overview of the state-of-the-art.

# CHAPTER 6

# the administration
# of
# planned organizational change

Self-renewal approaches to administering change in schools are built upon (a) a clear and specific analysis of schools as organizations and (b) the role of administration in them. Experience and research have clearly indicated that such approaches require the active leadership of administrators if they are to succeed. This means that the administrator *must* be an advocate of the self-renewal point of view if it is to succeed in the organization. Organization Development and other self-renewal approaches to change cannot be purchased and installed in the organization by a benevolently neutral administrator. Therefore, the administrator who wishes to foster self-renewal in the organization should be sure that he clearly understands and is committed to the crucial elements of the point of view underlying the concept.

Key elements of the point of view are:

1. A Theory Y understanding of people and work.
2. Various macro change strategies may be used in support of a humanistic educational organization. The choice among these strategies is not *either-or:* though they are often described in taxonomies as being disparate, the practicing administrator needs to synthesize and integrate elements of all of these strategies as we have discussed in chapter 4.
3. Change does not result from things that administrators do to people; it results from helping people—individually and in work groups—to identify organizational problems and to solve them. Organizational structures are created to facilitate this problem-solving orientation by opening communication and providing opportunities for involvement

in the problem-solving processes. The thrust is toward the development of a more organic organization.

4. Social systems views of organization preclude partial, limited, or piece-meal concepts of organizational change. The organizational factors involved in change (task, technology, structure, people) are highly interdependent, rather than isolated from one another.

## BASIC CONSIDERATIONS
## FOR ADMINISTERING CHANGE

The administrator who wants to develop a program of planned organizational change must first develop some fundamental skills, knowledges, and attitudes. Secondly, he must think through his own role as a guide to action. Thirdly, he must clarify for himself the strategic elements that are essential to an effective plan for action.

### Required Skills, Knowledges, and Attitudes

Thus far, we have been discussing a generalized orientation to and understanding of essential conditions for organizational change. We turn now to consider, in more specific terms, the kinds of skills, knowledges, and attitudes that are required of educational leaders in order to deal successfully with problems of implementing planned organizational change.

First, consider the present and future role of educational administrators in terms of what skills it suggests are needed. Data from survey research reported by the Oregon School Study Council[1] suggests that high school principals and professors of secondary school administration generally feel that in the future the high school principalship will emphasize the following roles: (1) instructional leader, (2) systems specialist, (3) planner, (4) coordinator, and (5) change agent. Among the special competencies projected as necessary for administrators in the future are (1) skills in developing evaluative criteria, (2) interpersonal skills, (3) conflict management, (4) community involvement, and (5) the ability to bring about instructional change.

The 1985 Committee of the National Conference of Professors of Educational Administration probably shared this view as they looked into the future. Being concerned primarily for the implications for programs to train educational administrators, their study called for the survival until 1985 of only those training programs that met the following

[1] Oregon School Study Council *Bulletin*, April, 1974.

criteria: (1) utilized the results of basic research on learning and organizational behavior and provided balanced emphasis among the social and behavioral sciences, (2) provided experience in dealing with social problems and with policy issues growing out of changing technologies and new capabilities for conditioning human behavior, (3) showed concern for individuals as such, for the attainment of individual goals, and for continuous evaluation of their performance and potential, and (4) gave training in the functioning of administrative teams and inculcated the value of shared accountability for results.[2]

To fulfill this promise of leadership the administrator must be capable of implementing appropriate strategies and tactics of organizational change from among those suggested by Havelock, Chin and Benne, and Katz and Kahn that were described in chapter 4. The best approach to the selection and implementation of change strategies and tactics will, undoubtedly, be morphogenic in nature—emphasizing self-renewal, a planned approach to improve organizational health, featuring adaptive organizational problem-solving. Basic to the approach will be the integration of training of work groups in such skills as communication and problem-solving with the usual ongoing activities of the school. The chief enduring outcome of such training is a self-renewing system that is ". . . motivated to monitor its own functioning and the changing environment, capable of assessing areas where change is suggested and flexible enough to modify its organizational form and functioning to meet its need effectively."[3] To provide this training for faculty and staff is, indeed, a challenge to the leadership of any administrator.

To meet the challenge successfully, the administrator must frankly consider whether he feels it necessary to play the role of mentor in his school—an all-knowing "teacher of teachers"—or whether he is prepared to continue learning, along with the faculty and staff. This involves careful consideration of how well-prepared the administrator is—not only in terms of skills, but also in terms of time and energy—to plan and conduct the needed training sessions, workshops, and other activities. It also involves an assessment by the administrator as to how ready he is to call upon specialists to assist in furthering his leadership by providing diagnostic services and organizational training for which he may not be specifically trained.

[2] Richard C. Lonsdale and Robert E. Ohm, "Futuristic Planning: An Example and Procedures," in Walter G. Hack, et al., *Educational Futurism 1985* (Berkeley: McCutchan, 1971), pp. 109–128.
[3] Daniel Langmeyer, et al., "Organizational Training in Sub-Systems of a Midwest School District," in William L. Claiborn, et al., eds., *School Intervention* (New York: Behavioral Publications, 1973), p. 193.

### The Administrator's Role in Planned Change

In the organic, self-renewing school the administrator's role is to "work with and through individuals and groups toward the goals of the organization," as we pointed out in chapter 2. This clearly emphasizes the complex task of leadership that seeks to involve the staff in identifying and solving problems they feel are important. It clearly deemphasizes the hierarchical tradition whereby ideas are born at the top and implemented by lower-level members of the staff. In administering planned organizational change, therefore, a major problem is to develop specific *practical* ways of doing this.

This is much more of an administrative problem than creating a committee structure in the school or setting up a task force or two. While these procedures typify aspects of the administrator's role as facilitator, it is necessary to provide the groups with specific training so as to develop their skills in organizational decision-making and problem-solving.

The administrator has two basic options that may be exercised in providing organizational skill-training to the faculty: (1) he may choose to provide the training himself or (2) he may elect to work with a specialist in organizational behavior. Many administrators find it desirable to work with a consultant specialist for two principal reasons: (1) there are frequent instances in the training of school faculties for organizational self-renewal wherein the administrator and the other members of the system are so personally involved in the situation that it is difficult for the administrator to assess the situation in an impartial way. In these instances a skilled neutral consultant can be helpful to both the administrator and the faculty in seeing things "as they are" and finding ways of improving them. (2) In other instances, even a well-trained administrator finds it productive to draw upon the knowledge and skills of a specialist consultant in dealing with especially difficult and complex training problems.

Some administrators tend to think that bringing in a consultant is an admission of professional weakness and means turning the leadership of the school over to an outsider. In fact, however, the decision to use a consultant in planning and carrying out organizational skill-training for the faculty is a relatively new option for exercising leadership. We contend that the administrator who out-of-hand rejects the option of using a consultant is also passing up an opportunity to engage in productive leader behavior. The administrator who knows when and how to use the services of a specialist consultant is opening up opportunities to exercise new and more powerful leader behavior. Other professions provide us with useful parallels. One's family physician, for example, would surely not be thought to be exhibiting incompetency if he called in a specialist to help in diagnosis and treatment when *in his professional judgment* the situation warranted it.

A further consideration in implementing change is the extent to which power and authority are shared with the staff. The "democratic administration" approach of earlier decades was unsuccessful largely because the endless committee meetings were generally correctly perceived by teachers to be "window dressing" and, in the end, the administrators were virtually all-powerful. The organic self-renewing school is characterized by a clearly established structuring of appropriately shared power and authority in decision-making. Indeed, the organization can only develop as the involvement of staff becomes increasingly more effective over time. The administrator should give thought to his own willingness to develop the self-confidence and the sophisticated explicit administrative and interpersonal skills required of him.

### Organization Development Plan for Change

Traditional approaches to administering change in schools have often emphasized staff development. Conventionally, this has included such techniques as close, detailed supervision and in-service training. Such an approach is based upon the conviction that a major barrier to goal achievement of the school is the inadequacy of the professional knowledge and skill of the individual teachers.

While the organization development concept of planned change does not rule out the importance of such skills, it stresses another dimension of staff performance: organizational skills. Thus, a basic consideration in the administration of change in schools is the training of staff in the skills that facilitate productive involvement in organizational process. This will include training in skills required for effective team membership, effective communications, interpersonal and intergroup functioning, and group problem solving.

Thus, the administrative thrust of organization development is to develop the skills of organizational participation that enhance the functioning of the school as an organization (e.g., diagnosing and solving problems that affect the goal achievement of the school as a total organization).

### Sociotechnical orientation

Administrators who are inexperienced in humanistic approaches to management often think of them as being "soft," "permissive," and incompatible with the structure, discipline, and power that characterize organizations. In fact, however, what is needed is a new, more effective, approach to management: an approach that stresses more functional administrative structures and seeks more effective organizational behavior. Although the new structures may well be more flexible and adaptable than those of the past, they will not be fuzzy or ill-defined; neither will the more effective work-related behaviors be lacking in clear, exact description and definition.

When the contemporary administrator confronts the need for more involvement of staff in decision making or seeks to move his organization in a more "organic" or self-renewing direction, does it mean that system, orderly procedures, and control must be abandoned? The answer is, of course, negative. In fact, quite the opposite is true: the need is to provide organizational structures that will enhance and facilitate the development of more adaptive decision-making styles to replace the rigid hierarchical structures characteristic of the mechanistic organization.

The shift in organizational system development, then, is not away from clarity, order, and control associated with traditional views of organizational structure toward an ill-defined, disorderly, laissez-faire administration. What is sought, administratively, is a new and more functional basis for *task* analysis, *structural* arrangements, selection and use of *technology*, and selection and professional development of individual *people* and groups of people on the staff.

The rationality of this view—that we call a sociotechnical orientation —becomes increasingly apparent when we acknowledge that technological change and innovation are likely to play an increasingly important role in organizational change in schools in the future. The function of the administrator, then, is to develop organizational structures that—while providing clearly for such imperatives as coordination of effort toward goal attainment—assure the development of more adaptive ways of integrating people, technology, task, and structure in a dynamic, problem-solving fashion (See Figure 6-1).

*Planning for action*

How can we analyze an organizational situation so that we may better understand how to deal with it? Force-field analysis has proven to be a useful analytic approach for both the researcher and the administrator.

Basically, this approach sees a social or organizational *status quo* as a state of equilibrium resulting from the balance between two opposing sets of forces. There are forces for change, sometimes called *driving forces* and these are opposed by forces for remaining unchanged, sometimes called *restraining forces*. When these force fields are in balance, as in

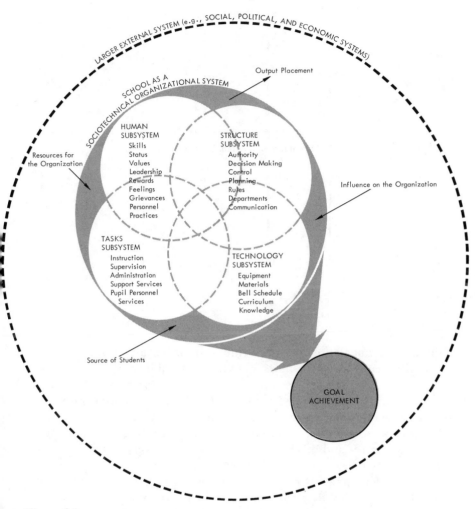

**Figure 6-1**
Four primary organizational sybsystems suggest the principal strategic orientations to organizational change.

Figure 6-2, we have equilibrium—no change. Obviously, when one or another of these forces is removed or weakened the equilibrium is upset and change occurs, as shown in Figure 6-3. On a very simple level, such an imbalance can be brought about by the introduction of a new work technique or the acquisition of new skills by participants. But an organization is essentially a stable entity generally characterized by equi-

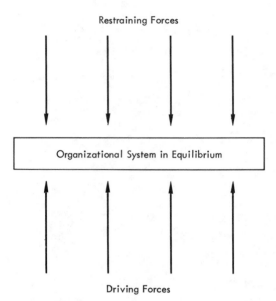

**Figure 6-2**
Force field in equilibrium.

librium; an imbalance of equilibrium will bring about readjustments that will again lead to a new organizational equilibrium. This simple concept can become very complex when applied to a large-scale organization. But it also can be a practical aid to the administrator who seeks to understand his organization better so as to facilitate either change or stability in the organization. The analytic process of identifying restraining forces and driving forces ranges from a very simple approach at the rudimentary level to rather sophisticated techniques.

Force field analysis eventually led Lewin to a fundamental three-step change strategy that has come into increasingly popular use.[4] It is predicated on the notion that in order to effect organizational change it is first necessary to break the equilibrium of the force field; that is, the organization must be *unfrozen*. Once that is done, it is possible to introduce *change*—to move the organization to a new level. But no one knows better than educational administrators how fragile change can be, how easily the organization can slip back into its old ways. Therefore, the third step in the three-step change process is *refreezing*. This is an institutionalizing process which serves to protect and insure the long-range retention of the change. Of course, refreezing smacks of a new

4 Kurt Lewin, "Frontiers in Group Dynamics," *Human Relations*, 1 (1947): 5–41.

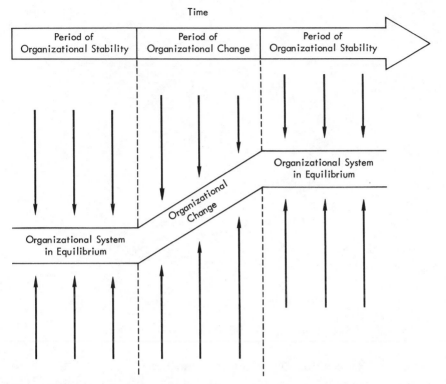

**Figure 6-3**
Imbalance of force field causes organizational change until a new equilibrium
is achieved.

status quo; in Lewin's view, the desired amount of flexibility could be
built in by establishing "an organizational set up which is equivalent to
a stable circular causal process." [5] Unfreezing can be a highly traumatic
experience to a very rigid and resisting organization. But it can also be
built in as a normal part of its life cycle, as suggested in Figure 6-4,
in order to achieve greater organizational flexibility over time.

The value of a force-field analysis is diagnostic: it permits the
preparation of plans for specific action designed to achieve the changes
sought. The success of such a plan will depend in large measure upon
the clarity with which the likely consequences of proposed action are
perceived. Of the four major organizational subsystems—task, technological, structure, and human—only the human subsystem has the capacity
to react differentially to differing conditions.

[5] Lewin, *Ibid.*, p. 35. The definitive work in this area by Lewin is *Field Theory
in Social Science* (New York: Harper and Row Publishers, 1951).

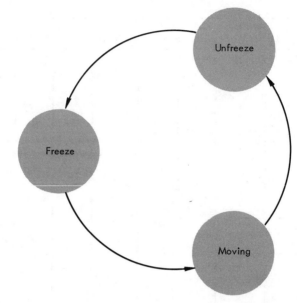

**Figure 6-4**
A three-step change as an ongoing life cycle of an organization.

Great art and literature teem with depictions of heroic achievements of people moved by such feelings as love, faith, courage, and duty. Much of the literature on organizations is concerned with apathy, anger, frustration, and apprehensions of people and their great power to inhibit the organization's goal achievement. While administrators must be deeply concerned with the work to be performed in the school, the structure of the organization, and the technology that is used, none of these has the capability of resisting plans for action. It is only the human subsystem which has that capability.

But it is not productive for the administrator to view opposition to change in any form—whether as outright resistance, apathy, skepticism, or whatever—as obdurate behavior.

If "increasing the driving forces" is interpreted by the administrator as meaning the stepped-up use of authority and power to get people behind the change effort, it is highly predictable that the result will be strong reactions against the change. Pressure generates counterpressure and in the school setting, where the administrator's coercive power is sharply limited, it is not likely that the equilibrium of the force-field can be broken by such an approach. At the very least, it is predictable that as the pressure is relaxed—as it must be eventually—there will be a tendency for the organization to retreat to its old ways under the pressure of the restraining forces.

In school situations generally it is likely to be more effective to help bring the restraining forces into the open as legitimate in the process of change. By creating a climate in which feelings can be expressed instead of secretly harbored, by opening communication and valuing the right to question and challenge, and by helping those who would oppose the forces of change to examine and deal with the concerns that cause their resistance, it is likely that (a) unforeseen probable consequences of proposed actions would be brought into the planning process and—perhaps more important—(b) the level of resistance will be diminished.

As the opposition contribute to shape and mold decisions, their views are also shaped, molded, and modified in the process. *To obtain this kind of participation requires the existence of a developmental, or growth-enhancing, organizational climate. This is a climate that characteristically*

   a. is intellectually, politically, and aesthetically stimulating.
   b. emphasizes individual and group achievement.
   c. places high value on the personal dignity of individuals.
   d. accepts divergent feelings and views in a nonjudgmental way.
   e. is oriented to problem-solving rather than winning or losing in intraorganizational skirmishes.

The establishment of orderly problem-solving processes that provide maximum participation for those who will be affected by the change is necessary to develop the collaborative approach suggested here. Although the point of view is important, it must be accompanied by effective specific procedures for making it work: creating the climate needed and assuring that the way in which decisions are reached is understood and workable. Development of a new organizational climate and building the group skills for open, collaborative decision-making requires definite training and practice. These things are not achieved through cognitive understanding and determination alone: they require the development of new insights, new values and commitments, and new group process skills that are best taught and learned in problem-solving situations.

It must be remembered that the creation of a new organizational climate—a new environment for working and solving problems—requires participants to develop new and more effective responses to events, to act differently than they have done in the past. As every educator is keenly aware, such changes in human functioning do not often occur as a result of learning *about* the new, more effective ways of doing things. Opportunities must be provided wherein the new behaviors may be developed in practice: in short, *learning by doing* is required. The goal is to develop new and more productive norms of work-oriented behavior through re-education.

The qualified consultant, skilled in the application of behavioral science to organizations should be especially helpful in this normative reeducation process. In chapter 7 we provide some guidelines and information that may be helpful to those who are interested in planning to use consultant services in organization development.

Change is likely to be stabilized and maintained in the organization over time when the new, more effective levels of performance can be maintained without coercion and without continuous expenditures of administrative energy and vigil to keep it going. Indeed, this is one practical criterion by which the administrator may judge whether or not change has been "accomplished."

An appropriate plan for organizational change must take cognizance of these realities. It must also recognize that the goal of changing an organization in significant ways presents a challenge in terms of difficulty and in terms of the time span required. There are no quick and easy solutions, though there will probably never be a shortage of those who claim to possess such solutions. Hersey's and Blanchard's admonition on this point is highly appropriate:

> Changes in knowledge are the easiest to make, followed by changes in attitudes. Attitude structures differ from knowledge structures in that they are emotionally charged in a positive or a negative way. Changes in behavior are significantly more difficult and time consuming than either of the two previous levels. But the implementation of group or organizational performance change is perhaps the most difficult and time consuming.[6]

## THE SELF-RENEWAL PROCESS

While the technology of OD is sufficiently sophisticated and diverse to permit the use of a wide variety of intervention and training techniques, there is an overall orderly process involved in using it to develop self-renewal capability in the organization. As shown in Fig. 6-5 the process includes a number of specific and clearly identifiable stages that flow into one another in a sequence of events. In managing an OD project it is important to (1) provide for each stage in the process to be fully

---

[6] Paul Hersey and Kenneth H. Blanchard, *Management of Organizational Behavior*, 2nd ed. (Englewood Cliffs, N.J.: Prentice-Hall, Inc., 1969), p. 3.

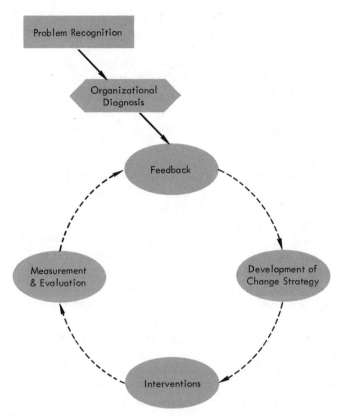

**Figure 6-5**
A model of the Organization Development process. From *Organization Development: A Reconnaissance* (New York: The Conference Board, Inc., 1973), p. 6.

implemented and (2) to be sure that no stage in the sequence is skipped or neglected. Thus, the schema shown in Fig. 6-5 can be useful to the administrator in coordinating and controlling the enterprise. As in any effort to flow-chart a complex administrative task, we run the risk of oversimplifying here. In actual school situations, of course, each of the specific stages is not necessarily fully completed before the succeeding stage is begun; often there is some overlapping. But the point stressed here is that the administrator should have a clear and orderly concept of what the OD self-renewal process is, what its major elements are, and what the sequence of events should be.

*Problem recognition* refers to the stage at which the organization becomes aware that it has a problem and wants to do something about it. At this point, the nature of the problem may not be well understood:

to some it may be experienced as a general discomfort or sense of organizational malaise. Others may ascribe various causes to the problem. Frequently, the problem is associated with some crisis facing the organization, such as reorganization, public criticism, or evidence of low goal achievement. Until the organization recognizes that it has a problem, however, there is little that can be done to help in the way of an OD effort. The administrator can, of course, do a great deal to either enhance or inhibit the processes of recognizing and confronting organizational problems.

*Organizational diagnosis* is the stage in which the problem is examined and defined; the diagnosis is always based on data. Very often at this stage the consultant seeks information from people in the organization, as well as material from the files. He uses observations, interviews, and questionnaires to obtain the views, feelings, and concerns of people in the organization. Techniques are being developed, however, that enable participants to learn to conduct their own organizational diagnoses with little or no consultant assistance.

*Feedback* and analysis of diagnostic data are used to involve the participants in the process of recognizing the organization's problems, diagnosing them, and planning to do something about them. The diagnosis and feedback stages often overlap and/or reciprocally feed into one another over time.

This stage of OD is ripe with opportunities to train a group, such as a school faculty. This training need not be confined to techniques for gathering diagnostic data and feeding them back to participants in appropriate ways. It can also be focused on such things as group process skills, communication techniques, and goal setting.

*Development of change strategy* is based upon the group's perceptions of what is needed in order to reduce the discrepancy between what should be and what is actually happening in the organization. Because the development of a change strategy can be complex and involve many variables, consultant help is often thought to be advisable at this stage. The planning should, however, deal with such specifics as (1) what steps will be taken, (2) by whom, (3) when, and (4) how effectiveness of the plan will be evaluated.

Again at this stage there are opportunities to engage the group in training. The skilled consultant working with a group at this stage is careful to provide a model of productive kinds of behavior as a member of the group and to seek ways to use the knowledges and skills that have been developed during earlier stages of the process.

*Interventions* may be designed to involve any or all of the basic organizational subsystems: that is, an intervention may be designed to deal primarily with the technology, the structure, the tasks, or the human social system of the school—or any combination of them. Because people play such a key role, virtually every OD intervention includes an important element for dealing with problems of the social subsystem. This often emphasizes trust-building, improving communication, team-building, group problem-solving skills, and developing collaborative (instead of competitive) relationships.

*Measurement and evaluation* means implementing the evaluation plan that was built into the process when the change strategy was designed. Too often in OD this has been given insufficient attention, resulting in an inability to determine whether or not the interventions actually accomplished their goals. One common form of evaluation is to repeat the earlier diagnostic observations, interviews, and questionnaires. It is, of course, desirable to use systematic pre and post data-gathering techniques and make sure that the data used actually measure the variables that were addressed during the process. An even stronger evaluation design would be to treat the OD group as an experimental group and evaluate the results in relationship to the performance of a control group.

But measurement and evaluation in OD are not used merely to determine the effectiveness of the process in objective terms. The new data are useful as feedback to the group, thus completing the cycle of events in the OD process and, in turn, initiating a new cycle of events. This cyclical process, once established and institutionalized in the organization, becomes never-ending, and this is the mechanism for organizational self-renewal that OD seeks to build into the organization.

This process is precisely the one that most schools lack or have only partially developed. It is the process that must be created, nurtured, and coordinated by those who are interested in administering change in schools.

### Central Role of the Administrator

There is a widely held view that planned interventions for change are developed and applied to organizations by experts who are outside of the organizations themselves. This is directly contrary to an important reality of schools. It is true that even administrators who are very influential will on occasion seek some outside consultant to help the school in redirecting its functioning in desirable ways. However, unless the administrator is directly involved as a central figure in making decisions, diagnosing problems, and launching new processes, such efforts are at best doomed to be peripheral. Potentially, at least, the administrator is in an enviable position to function as a change agent.

The central figure in planned change is the administrator. Few efforts to change significantly the course of organizational events will succeed over his opposition or in the face of his indifference. Certainly, it is difficult to picture achieving the goals and values of OD in any deep sense without the administrator's active involvement in clarifying issues, sorting out the options, making decisions, committing resources, and coordinating the necessary activities. If the OD effort is to be more than superficial and temporary—if it is to affect the central policies and practices of the school organization—then the intervention must become an important part of the administrator's job responsibilities.

The central role of the principal in determining the effectiveness of elementary schools, for example, was underscored by a study of two matched urban schools in which one school consistently out-performed the other in reading achievement tests.[7] The only clearly discernible difference between the schools was the leader behavior of the two principals. In the high-achieving school (School A), reading had been identified as an important problem, the faculty knew this and supported the clearly defined plan that had been developed to deal with it; the principal and the assistant principals had developed a clear plan to provide leadership and support to the classroom teachers in improving reading instruction, and the teachers felt that it was helpful; and, finally the climate in the school was generally supportive of learning.

The low-achieving school (School B)—although similar to its high-achieving counterpart in many ways—presented quite a different picture. Teachers there were pessimistic about improving reading achievement and were confused as to the priorities in the school. There was no clearcut plan to provide instructional leadership or support for classroom teachers. The climate was characterized by apathy, absence, disruption, and failure. The behavior of the principals of these two schools, as they attempted to provide leadership, was remarkably different: the principal of School B (low-achieving school) was apparently being guided by classical/mechanistic views, whereas the principal of School A (high-achieving school) revealed a nice balance of concern for structure and concern for people.

This is an interesting case in terms of planned organizational change if one raises the question, "Can School B be improved?" Considerable improvement might well result in such a situation if the principal of School B could enhance his leadership by initiating a program of organizational skill-training aimed at improving communication, problem-solving, and related group-functioning processes. Without such leadership on his part, however, it is unlikely that significant change would occur.

7 *School Factors Influencing Reading Achievement: A Case Study of Two Inner City Schools* (Albany, New York: State of New York, Office of Education Performance Review, March 1974).

## OD is a Line Administrative Function

To have maximum impact on the organization—indeed, tc be centrally relevant—OD must be accepted as a line administrative responsibility. There is some difference of opinion as to whether the acceptance of this responsibility is a prior condition that must exist before an OD intervention can succeed or something that may be developed later as the OD effort matures.

Some organization specialists believe that OD virtually demands that the top administrators initiate the intervention. In the world of business, for example, special conferences are arranged in posh surroundings for various corporation presidents to gather and learn about the possibilities of OD. The thought is, of course, that these influential men may return to their firms and seek ways to apply the concepts. It is difficult to rebut the contention that an OD effort initiated at the top-level and bearing evidence of strong administrative support has a much rosier prospect for long-term success than one that does not.

Not all OD efforts can be initiated in this fashion, however. Not all schools and school districts are led by administrators who know much about OD or have much faith in it. Does this mean that OD cannot be implemented until their outlook changes or they are replaced? Some organization specialists would answer affirmatively, holding that the authority and influence of the administrator are so great that the likelihood of much success without his active support is not bright. Other organization specialists disagree with this view, contending that although initiation by top administration is highly desirable, it is possible to proceed effectively without it under certain conditions. Important among those conditions is that administration must support the goals of the change effort and commit itself to those goals in tangible ways.

Thus, in one situation a school district employed a principal for a proposed junior high school a year before it opened. The principal selected some key people—mostly department heads—and during the year the group worked with an OD consultant in setting goals and planning for the new school. By the time teachers were brought into the process (the summer prior to the opening of school), the planning and development process was expanded. Another enlargement of the OD effort came with the opening of the school, when it was decided to involve students and community people in the effort.

The superintendent of schools was so impressed with the achievements of the approach that he asked the consultant to meet with other principals in the district and discuss the OD project with them. In this way the superintendent—at first not wholly enthusiastic about the OD idea—served as a very positive link between the junior high school and other subsystems in the district. Because the target for change is the entire system (i.e., in this case the school district), this concept of establishing *linkages* between the subsystems as part of OD is crucial. Few people in school districts have greater influence over facilitating or inhibiting linkage between the subsystems than administrators.

### Approaches to Intervention Strategies

Organizational change requires that those who are members of the organization diagnose their situation and initiate appropriate action.

Organization Development specialists have developed a comprehensive schema that enables the administrator to understand more clearly the interrelationships between three factors: (1) the mode of OD intervention, (2) the human group upon which the intervention is focused, and (3) the diagnosis of organizational problems. The "OD Cube," as the schema is known, is a useful guide to intervention techniques and their application to specific organizational conditions (see Fig. 6-6).

Organizations, however, are not changed by outside experts, though under some circumstances they can help members of the organization achieve their goals. All OD interventions are based upon this simple truth that is widely ignored in organizations.

The OD intervention is intended not merely to solve a particular problem of immediate concern, but also to build into the organization some new skills in diagnosing and solving problems. This is the self-renewal concept and it implies that the intervention should not only help to solve one problem but should help those in the organization to identify and solve other problems. There are three general approaches to designing intervention strategies.

### 1. Finding an organizational theory frame of reference

This approach to OD planning requires that the administration take time to reexamine their concept of organizational behavior to see if it conforms with their administrative practice. Few administrative groups in American public schools take time to discuss seriously organizational theory, their system of values and philosophy of administration, as these things relate to what is going on in the schools. An examination of the differences between theory and practice in such terms as McGregor's Theory X and Theory Y, or Herzberg's motivators and hygiene factors, or Blake's Managerial Grid concepts can lead to (a) determination to close the gap between professed belief and action and (b) a search for ways of actually closing the gap.

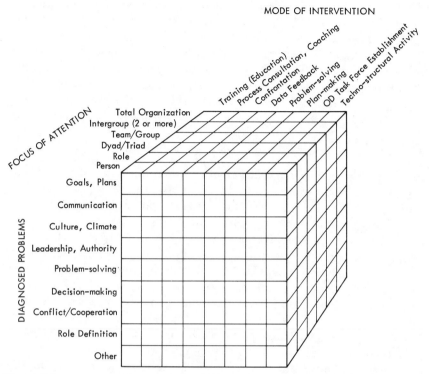

**Figure 6-6**
The OD Cube: a scheme for classifying OD interventions. Reprinted from
Richard A. Schmuck and Matthew B. Miles, *Organization Development in
Schools*, by permission of Mayfield Publishing Company, formerly National
Press Books. Copyright © 1971 by National Press Books.

## 2. Confronting the organization's problems

This general approach assumes that organization development depends
upon better diagnosis or analysis of the organization's problems. The
thrust is to identify significant problems—even those that were formerly
denied, ignored, or put aside—to search for basic solutions to them, and
to put the solutions to work. This means opening up communications
between people and groups in such ways that the attempt to identify and
diagnose problems leads to *real* problems rather than to generalities or
fictions.

Specifically designed groups can be set up for this purpose—such as
"rap" sessions and confrontation meetings. However, existing opportunities can also be utilized by upgrading the skills of those involved. Thus
ad hoc work groups and existing committees can be utilized creatively
to open up communication on organizational problems by improving

the group process skills of those involved. In American public schools the regular principal-faculty conferences offer a rich and rare opportunity for initiating OD through confronting problems. These encounters are frequently drab, uninspiring, routine: it is well-documented that teachers frequently feel that they are a great bore because they tend to deal with the wrong issues. *With support from the principal and the aid of a skilled organization consultant the principal-faculty conference in many schools could be quickly revitalized to make it a potent force for positive change.*

### 3. Exploring the systemic nature of the organization structure

The activities of this approach involve examining the structure of the organization and the interrelationship of its subsystems. Generally this requires the creation of face-to-face groups that may be permanent or temporary (e.g., task force or joint study group) to link the organization's subsystems. For example, school systems are commonly characterized by notably poor linkage (hence communication) between high schools and elementary schools; commonly, high schools within a district are often more noted for their remoteness from one another than for their productive interrelationships. The same condition often applies to elementary schools within a district and, indeed, *within* the schools themselves, as between the kindergarten teachers and sixth grade teachers. Structuralist approaches to OD envision building a network of effectively functioning linking groups in the organization. These serve not only to increase the variety and range of human resources brought to bear on problems but also can lead to the development of new organizational forms and structures better suited to the achievement of the organization's goals.

### SUMMARY

Self-renewing approaches to administering change in schools demand that the administrators commit themselves to a development point of view. This is predicated upon (a) a clear and specific understanding of schools as sociotechnical systems and (b) the role of the administrator in such systems. Although this point of view may be generally characterized as humanistic, its implementation in practice requires considerable specific administrative skill.

Our analysis of schools as organizations rests upon the application of behavioral science concepts and knowledge. The concepts and technology that underlie organization development are the basis for administrative practice and the administration of planned organizational change.

The essence of OD is learning. The central purpose of OD intervention is to improve the skills of those who are in the organization to diagnose and solve concrete, relevant, everyday problems. Thus, the processes of group problem solving are the focus of skill development. It is in "learning by doing" in the very practical sense that the people in the organization acquire new levels of skills in the process of dealing with on-the-job problems. A multiplier effect is built into the OD concept, for as a group succeeds in solving one problem it turns to other problems to see if they, too, are tractable to the new processes and skills being developed. Because individuals in one group are linked to other groups in the organization, the OD concept tends to spread through the total system.

## SUGGESTED READING

BECKHARD, RICHARD. "The Management of Organization Development." *Organization Development: Strategies and Models.* Reading, Mass.: Addison-Wesley Publishing Company, 1969. In a fifteen-page chapter the author briefly surveys the variety of approaches currently in popular use in the management of OD. Touches on possible roles of the administrator, uses of outside assistance, and use of internal change agents.

FRENCH, WENDELL L., and BELL, CECIL H., JR. *Organization Development: Behavioral Science Interventions for Organization Improvement.* Englewood Cliffs, N.J.: Prentice-Hall, Inc., 1973. This lucid, easy-to-read comprehensive description of OD authoritatively treats all major facets of the subject in considerable conceptual detail. Especially useful to the administrator who wants further information on concepts underlying OD strategies and techniques.

MELCHER, ROBERT D. "A School District Learns Its 3-R's by Clarifying Its ABC's." *Thrust* 3 (January 1974): 2–12. In this article the consultant whom the Anaheim (California) Union High School District selected to facilitate its development efforts describes the process that was utilized and some of the tangible changes that resulted. With an introduction by the superintendent of the school district, R. Kenton Wines.

SCHMUCK, RICHARD A., and MILES, MATTHEW B., eds. *Organization Development in Schools.* Palo Alto, Calif.: National Press Books, 1971. An invaluable book of readings for the administrator who has some general knowledge of planned change. Much of the material is drawn directly from various OD efforts in schools supplemented by pertinent material extracted from the general literature on planned change.

SCHMUCK, RICHARD A., RUNKEL, PHILIP J., et al. *Handbook of Organization Development in Schools.* Palo Alto, Calif.: National Press Books, 1972. Prepared by a group of authors with considerable experience as consultants in OD interventions in schools, this book presents a compilation of the concepts and specific training procedures widely used by consultants for organizations of all kinds (not only schools). While particularly useful to the individual who has training responsibilities, it will interest administrators who wish to know what many consultants *do* when they work with an organization.

# CHAPTER 7

# the organization
# development consultant

The OD consultant is an individual who is especially qualified by specific training and experience to design, coordinate, and evaluate an OD intervention that applies behavioral science (a) to organizational change problems, (b) of an entire organization or a major segment of a large organization, (c) over a substantial period of time. The OD consultant deals with the *organization* as a client, and it is the organization that is the focus of his influence.

This is sharply different from small group development or team-building in a school or department that is sometimes called OD but is only a part of the overall OD process. An important function of the OD consultant is to deal with the linkages between the subsystems of the organization. This might include schools within a school district, departments within a large and complex high school, and school systems within a county or regional district. The OD consultant should also be capable of training members of the client organization to function as internal OD specialists.

In practical terms, the educational administrator needs an OD consultant who has the capability to design, plan, and manage a total, sustained program of self-renewal for a specific organization—generally a school or a school system. Ordinarily, such a person would be a behavioral scientist with extensive special training and experience in OD above and beyond his academic preparation as a scientist.

One should distinguish between the consultant who is recognized as having this ability and others who do not have the training and experience in OD work. The terms *OD trainer* or *OD specialist* sometimes refer to individuals who have the skills and experience that enable them to perform OD functions—such as conducting training and feedback sessions—that are only a *part* of the overall design and management of the project. Thus, the supervising consultant will often arrange for trainers to carry out certain phases of an OD project that he has designed and is managing, rather than to handle all of the activities personally. Unfortunately for the administrator, even such terms as "consultant," "trainer," and "specialist" lack precision in describing the abilities and qualifications of people who are involved in OD consulting work.

## INTERNAL V. EXTERNAL CONSULTANT

It is recognized that organizations committed to the ideas of Organization Development and organizational self-renewal have a need for two distinctly different kinds of consultants: internal consultants and external consultants.

### The Internal Consultant

The internal consultant is an employee of the organization whose job is to assist in helping the organization meet its self-renewal needs. Although this position was still relatively new in American school districts by the mid 1970s, a number of districts were experimenting with ways to establish such a position and staff it appropriately.

There are at least four levels of internal consultants that show evidence of becoming established in American school districts:

1. *The in-school consultant,* who may be a teacher, guidance counsellor, or other full-time employee of the school who has been especially trained to perform in the role of consultant. Establishing such a position, either as a full-time or part-time position, tends to institutionalize and regularize the position and its functions.

2. *The multi-school consultant* is a school employee who is specifically trained for the change-agent role and is assigned to serve the needs of more than one school.

3. *The OD consultant unit in a school district* is staffed with trained OD consultants who are available on call to meet the needs of schools and other administrative units in the district for consultation on organization development activities.

4. *The multi-district organization development unit,* as in a county or regional board of educational services, is staffed and budgeted to assist

cooperating school districts to execute their organization development projects and to train their own on-staff consultants.

There appears to be little question that, given the realities of the budgeting and financing of American school districts, the concepts of organization development and organizational self-renewal will not prosper unless the idea of internal change consultants on the regular payroll is widely accepted. By the mid 1970s there were a number of instances in which the arrangements described here were being practiced, encouraging the belief that the practice would spread.

### The External Consultant

The external consultant is not an employee of the school or school district but is retained on a temporary basis to facilitate the management of an organization development effort. Such a consultant, being external to the organizational system and presumably possessing a high level of skills, is in a unique position to help as an impartial, neutral party. Because most schools and school districts begin their OD efforts with the help of external consultants (and only develop an internal consultant capability at a later time) we shall discuss problems relating to the external consultant at this point.

Locating a consultant requires a certain amount of preliminary search and inquiry into the background of possible consultants. The wise administrator will approach more than one consultant in preliminary discussions before engaging one for a proposed OD project. This will enable him not only to assess the qualifications of the consultant but also to gauge how readily he and the consultant seem to establish a good working relationship.

## ESTABLISHING A WORKING RELATIONSHIP WITH A CONSULTANT

Essentially, the OD consultant views his relationship to the organization much as a therapist-to-patient relationship. The prospective client organization has encountered a problem and wants help; the fact that the client took the initiative in seeking help indicates at least *some* desire to do something about the problem. This is important to the consultant because, in his view, it is the client who must ultimately solve the problem: the consultant can do many things to help the client to see the problem more fully, understand it, and develop ways of dealing with it. But he cannot solve the client's problem by telling him what is wrong and what to do about it.

In early contacts with a prospective client organization, therefore, the consultant will try to estimate how effective he can be in this particular situation. This depends to a great extent upon how readily he can establish a mutual relationship of trust and confidence with the administrator who initiates the contact.

Each organization seems to discover its problems in different ways; and, indeed, each organization is a unique system with distinctive needs and characteristics. In exploratory discussions with a consultant the administrator should be frank and forthright in discussing the situation from his point of view. He should try to gauge the rapport he feels with the consultant: how free he feels in talking with him, and how much confidence he has in this consultant's being helpful to the organization.

It is especially important that the administrator understand that the consultant will strongly prefer to view the *organization* as his client—not the administrator. Thus, although the consultant will want the full support and involvement of the administration in the OD project, he will not want to be viewed by teachers as an agent employed by the administration to work *on them.* The consultant may work at different times and in different ways with groups and subsystems of the organization, but his target for change must be an entire organizational system or major subsystem. This means that at times the consultant must play the part of a neutral third party, especially in situations involving conflict and confrontation.

However, it is highly likely that the consultant will in time seek to develop changes in the views, philosophy, and behavior of administration at least as much as in the lower ranks of the organization. These changes will certainly be in the direction of (1) a more humanistic concept of man and the forces that motivate his behavior, (2) a shift in concepts of power, away from threat and coercion (no matter how skillfully masked) to collaboration and reason as the sources of organizational discipline, and (3) the development of humanistic-democratic values, *human* values, to replace the depersonalized mechanistic value system associated with classical approaches to organization and administration.

## The initial contact

Organization development cannot be purchased as a "program" or a "package." It is a heuristic process that will develop and grow under favorable conditions. There is much ambiguity in the client-consultant relationship at the outset and neither party—consultant or administrator—has precise knowledge of what the problems and goals are. Therefore both administrator and consultant must be flexible toward one another.

The establishment of a working relationship with an OD consultant typically has three distinct stages: *first,* there is an initial contact; *second,* an exploratory meeting; and *third,* a contract, either explicit or implied, is agreed upon. Although there can be many local variables, there are some basic elements in all three of these stages that are important in the ultimate success of the proposed project.

The initial contact is always initiated by the organization. No matter how tentative, the decision to talk to a consultant reflects a recognition within the organization that it has problems and is seeking help in solving them. This initial contact can be highly informal: perhaps the superintendent meets a professor/consultant at a conference and broaches the subject to him. Or perhaps the superintendent simply wants to talk over the possibilities of OD with a consultant, calls one he has heard about, and arranges for him to come in for a brief discussion. The first contact can, of course, be made by persons lower in the organization's hierarchy—an assistant superintendent of personnel, for example, who knows a consultant through a professional association. The main function of the initial contact is to develop a mutual awareness that there is some common ground, and that both sides are open to further discussion. This sets the stage for the exploratory meeting.

## The exploratory meeting

The exploratory meeting involves a small, key group of people from the organization; selection of who should be invited is a sensitive matter and requires care. While some organizational specialists firmly hold that top administration must be involved with an OD project right from the start, this is probably not necessary. To a large extent it may depend considerably on the organizational climate in the particular school system and the resultant customs of the place. However, it is clear that it *is* highly desirable that the project have the active support of the superintendent throughout.

The group at the exploratory meeting should be (a) people who are concerned about and involved in the organization's problems and (b) generally favorably disposed to the idea that applied behavioral science techniques might be helpful. Openly hostile or aggressively skeptical people should not participate in the exploratory meeting: their presence at this stage serves merely to put the consultant on the defensive and makes it virtually impossible to establish a healthy relationship with the key group. At a later stage in the OD process it is possible to design other kinds of opportunities to work with hostility, conflict, and resistance.

In the exploratory meeting the consultant tries to become generally familiar with the situation, gauge the intent of those who invited him to come, and to establish through his own behavior what his role as consultant is to be. Most consultants feel that it is highly important that before committing themselves to a project there be a reasonable amount of openness on the part of the client's representatives regarding the organization's problems and aspirations and enough commitment by the administration to do something about them to assure support for a reasonable length of time. It is important, therefore, that the discussions be direct and candid at this time.

Although the initial client-consultant contact may have been brief—perhaps less than an hour—the exploratory meeting should provide more time for careful probing of problems, issues, and feelings involved in the situation. A half day devoted to this would not be excessive; more than this might be unnecessary. After all, what is sought is a decision: shall we heed this consultant's views and advice, or shall we look elsewhere? The answer depends to a great extent upon the chemistry in the situation; even a highly competent consultant can offer little to an organization if he does not get along well with key people, nor is he likely to involve himself if he feels that he will not have the confidence and cooperation of the people involved.

## The initial contract

After spending a half day or so discussing the situation with school administrators and perhaps other key people in the organization, the consultant should submit a brief letter of proposal for action that can be the basis for the initial contract. Such a proposal usually includes the following:

1. The stipulation that the consultant be employed by the client system for some minimum period of time on a per diem basis to initiate an organization development program.
2. A brief description of the early steps in the program. Normally these include (a) meetings with key groups to discuss plans, (b) the development of a plan for OD and its careful scrutiny by top administration, (c) the introduction of training activities in the system, and (d) a planned review of the project at a specified time (usually after at least six months) at which time the project can be terminated or adjusted.
3. A clear statement as to who the contact person is for liaison between the organization and the consultant. Communications and arrangements should be funnelled through this established contact only, so as to keep the lines of communication open and clear. Again it should be emphasized that this contact person is not the client: it is the *organization* that is the client. This simple but fundamental concept must be remembered.
4. A statement confirming at least in a general way the role and duties of the consultant. These include being a resource person who brings special knowledge, process skills, and diagnostic capabilities to the organization and acts as a facilitator to decision-making groups.

5. A statement of the consultant's per diem fee together with a flexible estimate of the number of days for which his services would be required during the duration of the project.

*Defining a client-consultant relationship*

Having established a simple agreement to work together, the next phase of the relationship—during the beginning stages of the OD project itself—is one in which the two parties seek to clarify and test its usefulness. The consultant gets a clearer view of what the client's hopes and expectations *really* are, as the client learns more accurately what the consultant expects of the relationship.

This may be illustrated by the case of a private school that faced a difficult major decision in redefining the school's fundamental purposes and goals and planning its future development. In an initial meeting involving the chairman of the board of trustees, the headmaster, and a representative of the parents' group it seemed clear that there was substantial agreement that their overriding need was to develop better communication and planning between teachers, students, parents, and trustees. An exploratory meeting with representatives of the board of trustees, the parents' group, and the teachers seemed to confirm this and the consultant agreed to work with the group, with the headmaster as the contact person.

The consultant team spent a day at the school working with the teachers and headmaster, followed by sessions designed to involve them in diagnosing problems and their feelings about them. Later, the consultant team worked with the board of trustees and members of the parents' group with similar purposes in mind. Following a second session with the teachers—that had been focused on developing some new alternatives to communication problems—the headmaster invited the consultants for tea, which was a custom of the place. It was at this time that the consultants became acutely aware that the headmaster expected "inside" reports on the beliefs and views of certain teachers whom he suspected of being in secret communication with the chairman of the board of trustees about him, the headmaster.

It was not long before the chairman of the board of trustees "happened to be in the neighborhood" of the consultants' office one day and stopped by to take them to lunch: it soon became evident that he was seeking confirmation of certain "rumors" that he had heard about the headmaster that raised some doubts in his mind as to his capability to deal with the school expansion that was being contemplated.

In this particular case it was possible to use the incidents as part of the diagnostic process and to work constructively on the problems that they revealed. Thus, the expectations of both the consultants and the client—unwritten expectations, but very real—could be met.

In many instances, however, the consultant finds that the expectations of others in the relationship may be so disparate from his own that it is in the best interest of everyone involved to terminate the relationship. It can easily happen that key people in the client organization will feel disappointed with a consultant, feeling that he is not doing what needs to be done—such as a principal who is bent on individualized instruction and wants the consultant to support the idea, or the superintendent who wants an expert opinion on a technical problem, or, indeed, a representative of the teachers' union who is virulently antiadministration and interprets any display of impartiality as antiunion. The consultant will normally try to identify such expectations early in the process and try to deal with them openly, often by attempting to clarify his own expectations and role with others in the relationship.

Perhaps one of the factors that a consultant dreads most in his relationship with a client organization is a lack of commitment or, worse, resistance. A willingness to explore problems, to take time to diagnose them, and to be generally supportive of the *effort* to help improve the organization in its performance and goal-achievement is essential to present concepts of OD. Frequently, those who have hostile attitudes toward efforts to improve the organization that do not necessarily meet with their approval seek to embarrass the consultant—insisting that he provide specific solutions to complex problems and, frequently, demanding *proof* of their validity. Pressed with sufficient vigor, such demands render the consultant's role untenable. Rather than a consultant on *process* who is prepared to help the client organization diagnose its problems and work out solutions to them—a neutral facilitator whose client is the *entire* organization—he is pressed to become an advocate of specific courses of action and a partisan in the internal politics of the organization.

Unless they can achieve an acceptance of their role as having primary focus on *process issues*—such issues, for example, as how the organization makes decisions, sets agenda, and gets work done—most consultants tend to conclude that there is little reason for attempting to continue the client-consultant relationship.

## COSTS OF ORGANIZATION DEVELOPMENT

Part of the organization's responsibility in an OD effort is, of course, to provide the resources necessary to carry out its commitment. This involves not only meeting the per diem fee of the consultant for whatever number of days has been tentatively agreed upon, but also providing the wherewithal to act upon suggestions and recommendations that the consultant might make as the OD process unfolds. Since an OD intervention must be planned in a purposively flexible way, so as to permit and encourage changes and developments over time, it is not possible to develop a rigid and precise budget beforehand. However, the budget for the project is something that should be discussed with the consultant very early so that the client will have a very clear picture of the costs that may be involved in the predictable future of the project. One of the obvious costs is the consultant's fee.

*Consultant fees* are widely variable. Well-known consultants can, and do, command several hundred dollars a day—and more—from corporate clients. The rate in public school organizations tends to be markedly less, owing to the realities of the situation. As a rule of thumb, the administrator should expect to pay a well-established consultant at least $150 per day. This can be revised downward in some cases: primarily where (a) the project promises to be of unusual research interest to the consultant or (b) there is an unusually long-term or high saturation commitment involved.

Many school administrators have had limited experience in dealing with consultants and, as a consequence, are unsure about the ethics and niceties of paying them. Since the preponderance of OD consultants are university professors, some administrators tend to believe that they should be pleased to come out and discuss a possible project with no fee involved; indeed, many consultants will do that whenever possible. It should be borne in mind, however, that consultation is a professional service: the most precious asset of the consultant, next to his expert knowledge, is time. It should be understandable, therefore, that an invitation to a consultant to discuss the possible need for his services incurs a certain responsibility. Many consultants do not expect to charge clients for an initial discussion to explore a possible OD project. Most, however, would justifiably expect to be reimbursed for meetings subsequent to that.

At the contract stage, which was described earlier, the wisest course is to discuss budgetary considerations very plainly with the consultant. It is more realistic and practical to design a modest project within the reach of a client than to proffer suggestions that will later turn out to be unrealistic. If the resources available are totally inadequate for an effective project, it would be better to face the fact early and plan another course of action.

*Incidental costs* of organization development also vary depending upon the extensiveness of the project, certain concepts and orientations, and the extent of the client organization's commitment. One of the primary sources of cost is *time.*

As long as OD efforts are limited to full-time administrators and supervisors—that is, those whose daily schedules can be arranged flexibly

—time can usually be found for the necessary meetings and activities. When teachers are involved, however—as they almost invariably should be—there is an administrative and a cost problem. It is unrealistic to believe that a meaningful OD project can be squeezed into time that teachers might voluntarily give—after school, evenings, during holidays, or on Saturdays. If there are to be discussions, meetings, planning sessions, or training opportunities involving teachers, then the client organization must assesses realistically its willingness and ability to provide for this. As the project widens to include students and parents the cost will rise.

Of course, scheduled conference days that have already been incorporated in the school district calendar provide *some* time for this. If the group of teachers involved is somewhat limited, costs might be restricted to the per-diem rate of substitute teachers. Where it is necessary to schedule activities on nonschool days, such as weekends or after the school year, the workable arrangements will have to be determined and budgeted.

## SUMMARY

Organization Development requires a consultant who possesses the skills necessary to design and facilitate the self-renewal process. There is much to be said for having an internal consultant—that is, a trained person who is an employee of the organization and who spends much or all of his time as a consultant to units of the organization. Such an individual tends to be familiar with the situation, knows key people, and is readily available. On the other hand, the internal consultant is subject to the expectations of the administrative hierarchy and lacks the third-party neutrality generally associated with the consultant role.

The external consultant is often widely experienced with many kinds of organizational problems, possesses a certain desirable neutrality and independence, and may be selected mainly for special skills relevant to a particular need of the organization. To marginally funded school districts, the external consultant appears to be expensive due to the fees that must be paid for his services, that may not be included under such line items in the budget as salaries.

Probably the optimum arrangement for a school interested in developing an organizational self-renewal capability is to undertake the training of some existing personnel as internal consultants with the assistance of highly qualified external consultants. In time, the school will have increased its own renewal capability but would still use external consultants to help with especially difficult design and training problems.

In any case, the ability of the consultant to be effective depends not only upon his skill and knowledge but also upon the working relationship that has been established with the administrator. For many administrators this kind of relationship is an unfamiliar one and, therefore, warrants careful exploration and explicit understandings by both parties. Perhaps the most difficult aspect of dealing with a consultant lies in understanding who the client is and understanding the unique role of the consultant in the context of the usual line-and-staff organizational concepts. These concerns are best handled by clear, forthright discussion leading to explicit agreement between the administrator and the consultant.

## SUGGESTED READING

DUFFIN, RICHARD; FOLUSI, ARNOLD; LAWRENCE, PHILIP; and MORTON, ROBERT B. "Increasing Organizational Effectiveness." *Training and Development Journal,* April 1973. Describes the structure and activities of the Organization Development Unit of the York County Board of Education, Aurora, Ontario over a three-year period. Focuses on selected concrete administrative problems related to budget decisions that were particularly addressed during that time. See also, by these authors, "Organization Development: What's It All About?" *School Progress,* September 1972. "Problems Can Only Be Solved from the Inside." *School Progress,* October 1972.

LOUSER, JAN J., SPIERS, HERBERT, and MOODY, CAROLYN. *The York County Board of Education: A Study in Innovation.* Toronto, Ontario: The Ontario Institutes for Studies in Education, 1972. Describes the purpose, functions, methods, and outcomes of a major pioneer Organization Development effort in a school district.

SCHMUCK, RICHARD A. and RUNKEL, PHILIP J. "Integrating Organizational Specialists into School Districts." Paper presented at the NTL Invitational Conference on New Technology in OD, New York, N.Y., October 8, 1971. Recounts the experience of two external consultants in establishing cadres of internal specialists in the school districts of Kent, Washington, and Eugene, Oregon.

# selected bibliography
# on
# organizational development

BECKHARD, RICHARD. *Organization Development: Strategies and Models.* Reading, Mass.: Addison-Wesley Publishing Company, 1964.

BENNIS, WARREN G. *Organization Development: its Nature, Origins, and Prospects.* Reading, Mass.: Addison-Wesley Publishing Company, 1969.

BENNIS, WARREN G., BENNE, KENNETH D., and CHIN, ROBERT, eds. *The Planning of Change. Readings in the Applied Behavioral Sciences.* 2nd ed. New York: Holt, Rinehart and Winston, 1969.

BLAKE, ROBERT R., and MOUTON, JANE SRYGLEY. *Building a Dynamic Corporation Through Grid Organization Development.* Reading, Mass.: Addison-Wesley Publishing Company, 1969.

BUCHANAN, PAUL. "Laboratory Training and Organization Development." *Administrative Science Quarterly* 14 (1969):466–80.

BURKE, WARNER W., ed. *Contemporary Organization Development.* Washington, D.C.: Learning Resources Corp., 1972.

BURKE, WARNER W. and HORNSTEIN, HAROLD A. *The Social Technology of Organization Development.* Washington, D.C.: Learning Resources Corp., 1972.

BUSHNELL, DAVID C. and RAPPAPORT, DONALD, eds. *Planned Change in Education: A Systems Approach.* New York: Harcourt Brace Jovanovich, Inc., 1971.

DOLL, RUSSELL C. et al. "Systems Renewal in a Big-City School District: the Lessons of Louisville." *Phi Delta Kappan* 54 (April 1973):524–34.

DUFFIN, RICHARD et al. "Increasing Organization Effectiveness." *Training and Development Journal* 27 (April 1973):37–46.

DUFFIN, RICHARD; FALUSI, ARNOLD; and LAWRENCE, PHILIP. "Organization Development: What's It All About?" *School Progress,* September-October, 1972.

*Educational Technology,* XII, No. 10 (October 1972) was a special issue devoted to "Organizational Development in Schools." Edited by Arthur Blumberg, it is an invaluable resource. Authors include Buchanan, Derr, Schmuck, Lippitt, and Havelock. Copies may be ordered at $3.00 each from *Educational Technology,* Englewood Cliffs, N.J. 07632.

FORDYCE, JACK K. *Managing with People: A Manager's Handbook of Organization Development Methods.* Reading, Mass.: Addison-Wesley Publishing Company, 1971.

FRENCH, WENDELL L. and BELL, CECIL H., JR. *Organization Development: Behavioral Science Interventions for Organization Improvement.* Englewood Cliffs, N.J.: Prentice-Hall, Inc., 1973.

GOLEMBIEWSKI, ROBERT T. *Renewing Organizations.* Itasca, Ill.: Peacock Publishers, 1972.

GROSS, NEAL, GIAQUINTA, JOSEPH B., and BERNSTEIN, MARILYN. *Implementing Organizational Innovations.* New York: Basic Books, Inc., 1971.

HAVELOCK, RONALD G. *The Change Agent's Guide to Innovation in Education.* Englewood Cliffs, N.J.: Educational Technology Publications, 1973.

HAVELOCK, RONALD G. and HAVELOCK, MARY C. *Training for Change Agents: A Guide to the Design of Training Programs in Education and Other Fields.* Ann Arbor, Mich.: Center for Research on Utilization of Scientific Knowledge, Institute for Social Research, The University of Michigan, 1973.

HAVELOCK, RONALD G. et al. *Planning for Innovation Through Dissemination and Utilization of Knowledge.* Ann Arbor, Mich.: Center for Research on Utilization of Scientific Knowledge, Institute for Social Research, The University of Michigan, 1971.

JOHNSON, DAVID W. "Evaluating Affective Outcomes of Schools." From H. J. Walberg, ed. *Evaluating School Performance.* Berkeley: McCutchan, 1974.

JONES, GARTH N. *Planned Organizational Change: A Study in Change Dynamics.* New York: Frederick A. Praeger, Publishers, 1969.

JOURNAL OF CONTEMPORARY BUSINESS, I, No. 3 (Summer 1972) was a special issue devoted to "Organization Development: an Overview." Authors include French and Bell, Blake and Mouton, Beckhard, Gibb, Burke, Shepard and Davis. An outstanding contribution to the literature for managers and administrators. Copies may be ordered at $2.50 from *Journal of Contemporary Business,* 135 Mackenzie Hall, University of Washington, Seattle, Washington 98195.

LANGMEYER, DANIEL; LANSKY, LEN M.; and REDDY, W. BRENDAN. "Organizational Training in Subsystems of a Midwest School District." From William L. Claiborn and Robert Cohen, eds. *School Intervention.* New York: Behavioral Publications, 1973.

LAWRENCE, PAUL R. and LORSCH, JAY W. *Developing Organizations: Diagnosis and Action.* Reading, Mass.: Addison-Wesley Publishing Company, 1969.

LEAVITT, HAROLD J. *Managerial Psychology.* 2nd ed. Chicago: The University of Chicago Press, 1954.

LIKERT, RENSIS. "Motivational Dimensions of Administration." Chapter 8 in Robert A. Walker, ed. *America's Manpower Crisis.* Chicago, Ill.: Public Administration Service, 1952.

LIKERT, RENSIS. *New Patterns of Management.* New York: McGraw-Hill Book Company, 1961.

LIPPITT, GORDON L. *Organizational Renewal: Achieving Viability in a Changing World.* New York: Appleton-Century-Crofts, 1969.

MANN, FLOYD C., and NEFF, FRANKLIN W. *Managing Major Change in Organizations.* Ann Arbor, Michigan: Foundation for Research on Human Behavior, 1961.

MARROW, ALRED J., BOWERS, DAVID G. and SEASHORE, STANLEY E. *Management by Participation.* New York: Harper and Row, 1957.

MARROW, ALFRED J. *The Practical Theorist: The Life and Work of Kurt Lewin.* New York: Basic Books, Inc., 1969.

MELCHER, ROBERT D. "A School District Learns its 3-R's by Clarifying its ABC's." *Thrust* 3 (January 1974):2–12.

MILES, MATTHEW B., ed. *Innovation in Education.* New York: Teachers College Press, 1964.

"O.D. at Saga." One of a collection of pamphlets in the packet, *Organization Development and the Saga Way.* Available from: William J. Crockett, Vice President for Human Resources, Saga Administrative Corporation, 1 Saga Lane, Menlo Park, California 94025.

ORLOSKY, DONALD and SMITH, B. OTHANEL. "Educational Change: Its Origins and Characteristics." *Phi Delta Kappan* 53 (March 1972):412–14.

OWENS, ROBERT G. "Change in an Organizational Setting." Chapter 7 in *Organizational Behavior in Schools.* Englewood Cliffs, N.J.: Prentice-Hall, Inc., 1970.

OWENS, ROBERT G. "Conceptual Models for Research and Practice in the Administration of Change." *Journal of Educational Administration* Vol. 12, No. 2 (October 1974): 4–17.

PINCUS, JOHN. "Incentives for Innovation in the Public Schools." *Review of Educational Research* 44:113–44.

PRETE, ANTHONY. *Reducing Alienation and Activism by Participation.* Columbus, Ohio: Ohio Education Association (no date).

ROGERS, CARL R. *On Becoming A Person.* Boston: Houghton Mifflin, 1961.

ROGERS, EVERETT M. *Diffusion of Innovations.* New York: The Free Press, 1962.

SARASON, SEYMOUR B. *The Culture of the School and the Problem of Change.* Boston: Allyn and Bacon, Inc., 1971.

SATUREN, STEVEN LEON. *On the Way to Adaptability: Some Conditions for Organizational Self-Renewal in Elementary Schools.* Ph.D. dissertation, University of Oregon, 1972.

SCHEIN, EDGAR H. *Process Consultation: Its Role in Organization Development.* Reading, Mass.: Addison-Wesley Publishing Company, 1969.

SCHMUCK, RICHARD A., and MILES, MATTHEW B., eds. *Organization Development in Schools.* Palo Alto, Cal.: National Press Books, 1971.

SCHMUCK, RICHARD A. "Bringing Parents and Students into School Management: A New Program of Research and Development on Organizational Development." *Education and Urban Society* 6:205–21.

SCHMUCK, RICHARD A.; MURRAY, DONALD; SMITH, MARY ANN; SCHWARTZ, MITCHELL; and RUNKEL, MARGARET. *Consultation for Innovative Schools.*

Eugene, Oregon: Center for Educational Policy and Management, 1975.

SCHMUCK, RICHARD A., RUNKEL, PHILIP J., and LANGMEYER, DANIEL. "Improving Organization Problem Solving in a School Faculty." *Applied Behavioral Science* 5 (Oct/Nov/Dec. 1969):455–82.

SCHMUCK, RICHARD A.; RUNKEL, PHILIP J.; SATUREN, STEVEN L.; MARTEL, RONALD T.; and DERR, C. BROOKLYN. *Handbook of Organization Development in Schools*. Palo Alto, Cal.: National Press Books, 1972.

SHERWOOD, JOHN J. *An Introduction to Organization Development*. Washington, D.C.: American Psychological Association, Inc., The Experimental Publication System, Issue No. 11.

STEELE, FRED I. *Physical Settings and Organization Development*. Reading, Mass.: Addison-Wesley Publishing Company, 1973.

TRIST, E. L. "The Causal Texture of Organizational Environments." *Human Relations* (February 1965):21–32.

WATSON, GOODWIN, ed. *Change in School Systems*. Washington, D.C.: National Training Laboratories, NEA, 1967.

———. *Concepts for Social Change*. Washington, D.C.: National Training Laboratories, NEA, 1967.

# index

173